BY THE NUMBERS

BY THE NUMBERS

FROM 00 TO 99

SCOTT MORRISON

WITH A FOREWORD BY DON CHERRY

CBCsports

KEY PORTER BOOKS

Library and Archives Canada Cataloguing in Publication

Morrison, Scott
Hockey night in Canada : by the numbers / Scott Morrison.

ISBN 978-1-55263-984-9

1. National Hockey League--Statistics. 2. National Hockey League-
-Miscellanea.
I. Title.

GV847.M67 2007   796.962'64   C2007-904763-7

THE CANADA COUNCIL | LE CONSEIL DES ARTS
FOR THE ARTS | DU CANADA
SINCE 1957 | DEPUIS 1957

ONTARIO ARTS COUNCIL
CONSEIL DES ARTS DE L'ONTARIO

The publisher gratefully acknowledges the support of the Canada
Council for the Arts and the Ontario Arts Council for its publishing
program. We acknowledge the support of the Government of
Ontario through the Ontario Media Development Corporation's
Ontario Book Initiative.

We acknowledge the financial support of the Government of
Canada through the Book Publishing Industry Development
Program (BPIDP) for our publishing activities.

Key Porter Books Limited
Six Adelaide Street East, Tenth Floor
Toronto, Ontario
Canada M5C 1H6

www.keyporter.com

www.cbcsports.ca

Text design and electronic formatting: First Image
End paper photo: Manor Photographic Imaging

Printed and bound in Canada

07 08 09 10 11 5 4 3 2 1

Acknowledgements

Funny, but it didn't seem like such a major undertaking the day the idea was first put on the table.

Or the day the deal closed.

But then, these things never do until you start to get at them, peel back the layers, fight all the logistical battles, get overwhelmed with normal daily duties (never mind the unseen hurdles), and begin to run out of time.

Which is a long-winded way of saying, to complete any publishing venture you need help. Lots of it.

There is no shortage of people to thank for this venture coming to fruition, beginning with *Hockey Night in Canada*'s executive producer, Joel Darling, who brought me into the fold a year ago and explored different ways to expand the *HNIC* brand and keep me busy. He had filed away an idea about a book about numbers, an idea that he and Ron MacLean had talked about. Next thing you know, I was putting together an outline and Jim Bennett was putting together the deal.

And then the fun began...

Not unlike the overall concept, the process of voting for the best player and top 10 players for each number didn't seem daunting until the ballots were assembled. That process started with the co-operation of the public relation departments of the 30 NHL teams, who either forwarded all-time roster and number computer files, or put them together and forwarded them. Either way, they came through big time and promptly.

From there, the unsung heroes went to work. Tony Care, from cbcsports.ca, and researcher Jenny Green went about creating 101 files—one for each number from 00 to 99—and distributing each team's information into the appropriate file. Not a lot of fun and not an easy task, but done thoroughly and well.

After all that was done, *HNIC*'s Anne-Marie Maugeri put together the ballots and got them out to the voters, then helped to hunt them down to be returned. Of course, this was all happening at the same time as the playoffs. Nice bit of timing, that.

Our cast of voters, who are to be sincerely thanked, included MacLean, Cassie Campbell, Scott Oake, Dick Irvin, Bob Cole, Kelly Hrudey, Jim Hughson, Greg Millen, Elliotte Friedman, and the Satellite Hot Stovers—Pierre LeBrun, Eric Duhatschek, and myself. Beyond that crew, we also had consultants to fill in the cracks: Don Cherry, Scott Bowman, Cliff Fletcher, Jim Robson, and Harry Neale.

After the voting was completed, Care took the ballots and assembled the results, giving each number a winner and, for the most part, a Top 10 list.

As for the 101 stories that had to be written, the quotes that had to be gathered and the fact boxes that had to be assembled, I had no shortage of help with the leg work. Because players were either finished for the year, or spread across the continent for the playoffs, getting background information and quotes wasn't easy. For that, thanks to the likes of LeBrun, Duhatschek, Oake, Friedman, Christine Simpson, Darren Dreger, Jeff Domet, Chris Johnston, Tim Davis, Jon Weatherdon,

Andrew Jackson, Ken Daniels, Carl Lavigne, and that group of public relations directors and NHL staff for suffering all the inconvenience and providing invaluable information.

Thanks to my former newspaper colleague, Patrick Grier, whose help was invaluable, as was that of Linda Pruessen and the gang at Key Porter.

A special note of thanks, of course, to all the players who shared their stories for this book. More importantly, though, these guys have given us countless hours of enjoyment on the ice over the years. Whatever the number, whatever the sweater, just to wear one in the NHL is something to be proud of.

Finally, thanks to a couple of key people on the home front—my son Mark, whose NHL draft is only a decade away, and my wife Kathy. As always, both were understanding and supportive when it was needed most.

— *Scott Morrison*

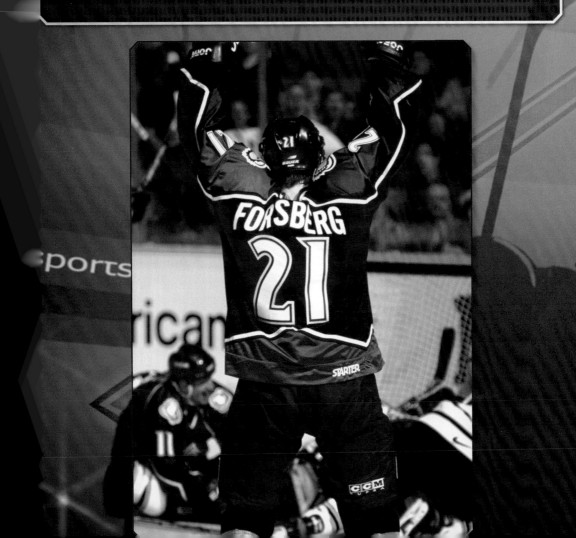

Foreword

Whenever I hear the number 4, I naturally think of Bobby Orr, the greatest.

On the other hand, early followers of hockey (especially around Montreal) would think of the great Canadiens centre, Jean Beliveau.

But that's part of what makes hockey special. We all have our favourites and we all have players we attach to a certain number, which is why I think this book is so interesting. It takes a look back at the players who wore different numbers, figuring out who was the best and why the guys wore the numbers they did. Years ago, remember, the low numbers were for goalies. Guys like Bernie Parent and Terry Sawchuk, they were number 1. And then the defense wore numbers 2, 3, 4, 5. If you ended up with number 6 it was not good [Author's note: Don was assigned number 6 for the one playoff game he played for the Bruins in 1955]. And if you were in the Boston organization and you were given the number 23, well, you'd better pack your bags—or don't unpack them, whatever the case. For some reason, guys who were given 23 did not hang around long. Nobody knows why. All I know is that number 23 was your ticket to the minors. It just was.

Number 9 was a big number, a special number, obviously with Gordie Howe, "Mr. Hockey," and of course "The Rocket," Maurice Richard. He chose number 9 because his daughter weighed nine pounds when she was born. And Gordie took 9 because it got him a better sleeping berth on the train. When I go and watch the young kids, the kid with 9 on his back is usually the captain, a centre, and a top scorer. That's just the way it is. Number 9 is the top number with the kids.

Some players, not many, just feel they must have a certain number and it really bothers them if they don't get it. I've had new guys ask me if someone would switch numbers with them. It took a lot of nerve to do that, but that was how sincere they felt and how important it was to them.

I played with the number 2 on my back, but a number meant nothing to me. Of course, I don't know if I go along with the people who say a number is nothing, like a rose would smell as sweet if it wasn't called a rose. Maybe, but Bobby Orr's first number in training camp was number 27. Just imagine the announcer saying, "Number 27, Bobby Orr," instead of "Number 4, Bobby Orr," the way we heard it all those years. It wouldn't have the same ring.

Anyway, almost every number brings back a memory for me and hopefully for you, too. And every number has a story.

Enjoy.

— *Don Cherry*

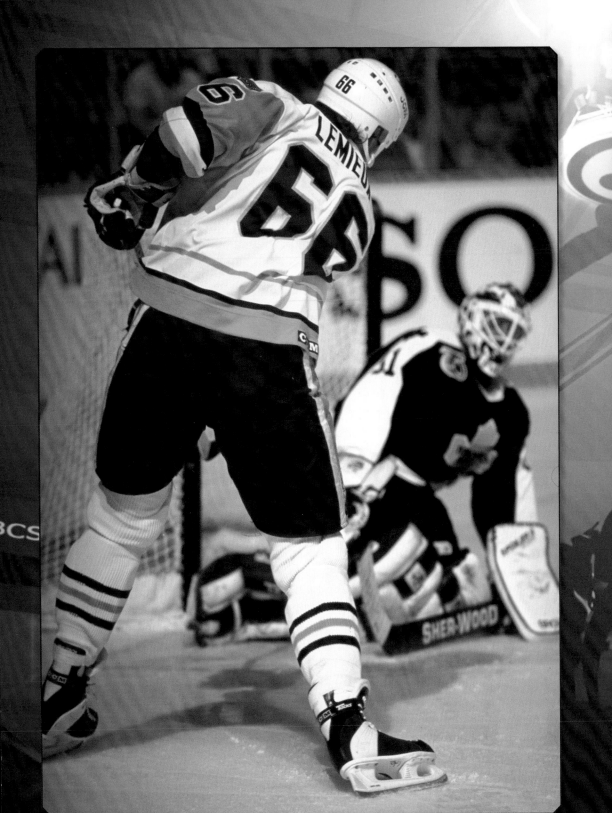

Introduction

In professional sports, it's all about the numbers: on the scoreboard, in the summary, on the contract—and on the back. It is also all about being the best, as a team and at your particular position.

This is true for baseball, soccer, basketball, and, of course, for hockey.

Given all of that, and understanding the hockey fan's undying passion and desire for debate, we at CBC's *Hockey Night in Canada* gave ourselves a task. We would determine the best of the best; we would take every number worn by a National Hockey League player—from double zero to 99—and figure out who was the greatest player to wear it.

For instance, who was the best ever to wear number nine? The list of contenders is long, from Gordie Howe to Maurice Richard to Bobby Hull to Andy Bathgate to Mike Modano to Ted Kennedy to Johnny Bucyk to Lanny McDonald to Charlie Conacher to Glenn Anderson to...

One could make a compelling argument for several of the selections, but ultimately everyone has his or her own opinion as to who is number one.

And so it goes.

With the help of an august group of hockey observers, we determined the best player to wear every number and, when applicable, nine runners-up. Not everyone will agree with the selections, of course, but then that is the essence of sport, the part about the passion and debate.

From the day that Guillaume Latendresse first wore the number 84 for the Montreal Canadiens, every single- and double-digit number has been worn in the NHL. In some cases, they have only been worn by one player. And in some cases, they have been worn in as few as two games (Mel Angelstad and the number 69). But every number has been filled and many players have worn multiple numbers throughout their careers.

Overall, this exercise was highly unscientific. Instead, it was designed to make hockey fans of all ages think a little, perhaps learn something and, hopefully, be entertained. Still, a few rules were put into place, but only a few.

One rule was that a player could only be declared the best at one number. This is why Howe couldn't be first with 9 and 17, why Hull couldn't win 7, 9 and 16, why Daniel Briere couldn't be first with 48 and 54, or why Terry Sawchuk couldn't take the honours for 1 and 30. It also explains why there are some unheralded winners in the more unusual digits.

By and large, to be declared a winner at a particular number, the player had to wear it for a reasonable length of time, though that criteria didn't necessarily apply to being a part of the accompanying list of runners up. While some winners are obvious, such as number 99, these lists are always interesting. It's fascinating to see who else wore the number, and to discover that Wayne Gretzky wasn't the first, second, or even third player to wear it.

Every rule, though, has its exception, and in some cases, winners were declared for numbers that they did not wear for the bulk of their career. Consider Scott Stevens. He didn't wear number 3 for all that long, but it was obviously enough to impact on the voters. (And speaking of the voters, we chose them pretty carefully—selecting both newcomers and veterans so we'd be sure to give the older players their due.)

In terms of the Top 10 lists and the team listed beside each player, various rationale was used to decide which club was most appropriate. It was often either where the player wore the number first or earned the greatest acclaim. It doesn't always reflect where an individual is playing now.

Finally, for the purposes of this exercise, we limited our selections to the NHL, meaning the likes of Vladislav Tretiak or Valeri Kharlamov did not make the cut.

The original lists of players from which we worked were garnered from information supplied by the 30 NHL teams. If you're reading a Top 10 list and don't see a name that you think should be there, it's because the voters didn't acknowledge it, which is their prerogative. If a name and number don't seem to jive and aren't registering on the internet, trust us, they were supplied by the team.

To say the least, this exercise wasn't as simple as it might have seemed at first blush. Selecting the best of the best is never easy—finding the right balance of time a player wore a number, how well he played, comparing different eras—well, it was tough but interesting.

Like I said, it wasn't scientific, but hopefully, it's provocative.

Hopefully, too, it will be entertaining. Whenever possible we have tried to tell the story behind the number, of why players wore the number they did, of why they changed, of the superstitions that inspired them in some cases and the indifference in others. There are a lot of cute and amusing stories attached to these numbers, stories which speaks volumes about the people wearing them.

Numbers are chosen for a million different reasons: to honour a parent, a hero, a political moment, a birth date, the birth of a child, to change bad luck. Others were simply told what to wear.

In some cases, players would ask for cash to surrender a number. In other instances, guys felt guilty enough about taking a number to buy gifts. Expensive gifts.

Did you know that while there are no shortage of numbers honoured or retired (the Minnesota Wild retired number 1 to honour their fans), there is only one number that is retired league-wide, though a couple of others have permanently been taken out of circulation.

The stories go on...

John Davidson

If he could do it all over again, chances are John Davidson wouldn't wear the number 00.

Of course, league rules prohibit any player from wearing zero or double zero these days, but Davidson wouldn't do it regardless.

"I have to admit it wasn't much fun going into visiting arenas," says Davidson, now president of the St. Louis Blues. "Especially as a goaltender. Fans came up with some classics, stuff like, 'We know 00 isn't your goals-against average, it must be your IQ.'

"The reason I wore it is because of Phil Esposito. When he got traded to the Rangers, he wanted number seven but Rod Gilbert had it. Phil asked me if I would wear 00 because he was going to wear 77 and at the time double digits were rare. Later on, when Ken Hodge got traded he wore 88 because Steve Vickers had eight.

"I was a naïve kid, 21 years old at the time, and I agreed to do it for him. Phil was the most superstitious player I ever met. In his dressing room stall he had all kinds of stuff hanging in there for good luck. But he wanted someone to help him with the transition to the new number and I was the guy."

Knee and back injuries plagued Davidson throughout his 10-year career, which began in St. Louis with the Blues drafting him fifth overall in 1973. Davidson became the first goaltender in league history to go directly from junior to the NHL full time. He was traded to New York in 1975

and, despite a bad knee, helped lead the Rangers to the Stanley Cup final in 1979.

After retiring, Davidson had a successful broadcasting career, won the Lester Patrick award in 2004 for service to hockey in the United States and was hired by the Blues as their president in June 2006.

Davidson and Martin Biron, with the Buffalo Sabres, are the only two NHL players to wear 00.

No. 00

1. **John Davidson,** New York Rangers
2. **Martin Biron,** Buffalo Sabres

Martin Biron

Bet You Forgot

As if Bernie Parent's talent as a goaltender wasn't intimidating enough, imagine what opponents thought when he came on to the ice sporting 00, the number he wore while playing with the World Hockey Association's Philadelphia Blazers in 1972-73. Not surprisingly, that year he led the league in both wins (33) and fewest goals allowed (220), though he only registered zeroes twice with two shutouts. He returned to the NHL the following season and led the Philadelphia Flyers to Stanley Cup victories in 1974 and 1975.

Bernie Parent

Neil Sheehy

Neil Sheehy was a hard-nosed defenceman with a good sense of humour. Apparently you needed one to wear a zero on your back.

A Harvard University graduate, Sheehy was signed by the Calgary Flames in 1983 as a free agent. He was part of the Flames team that went to the Stanley Cup finals in 1986 and had epic battles of Alberta with the Edmonton Oilers. Sheehy went on to play briefly with the Hartford Whalers, then the Washington Capitals, before returning to Calgary to finish his nine-season NHL career in 1992.

It was while playing in the minors with the Moncton Golden Flames that Sheehy first wore number 0.

"When I was with Calgary I had two games to go before my contract became a one-way contract," explains Sheehy, who has a law degree and became a successful player agent. "Calgary was on an eight-game losing streak and I got called into (general manager) Cliff Fletcher's office and told I was being sent to the minors (1985-86 season). That team was going to play four games in four nights on the road, what a treat.

"Terry Crisp was coaching the minor-league team at the time. When I got there, the trainer had a jersey with number 0 on it and he asked me what number I wanted. I said whatever, it didn't matter. He said would you do me a favour and wear this, number 0. I laughed and said absolutely. Crisp came in a few minutes later and said you're not going to wear that are you, and I said, sure. He laughed and said great, that's why I love you...

"So I wore it in the minors for four games. I got traded to Hartford in 1988 and when I got there I wanted number 5 because I had worn it before but it was taken. I had worn 15 before and it was taken. My first time in the minors I wore 21, but it was taken. So I asked the general manager, Emile Franics, if I could wear number 0. He looked at me funny and laughed, but I told him I wore it in the minors, Crispy loved it, and Emile said, 'why not?'

"When people asked me why I wore it I had some fun with it. I would tell them it was the furthest number from 99 and talent-wise I'm the furthest from Wayne Gretzky, but just remember opposites attract. At the time, the Battle of Alberta was pretty intense and my job was to play against Gretzky a lot of the time.

"I also told people I wanted to get the 'O' back in my name for O'Sheehy, my Irish ancestors. The truth is, in Ireland our name was MacSheehy. I just tried to have some fun with it. Fans used to yell at me, 'Is zero your IQ?' then somebody would say, 'Hey, this guy went to Harvard you know.' It was hilarious."

Sheehy was not regarded as being overly talented as a player, but was fiercely determined.

"His talent was average, but the reason he played nine seasons in the NHL is because of his fierce determination," says Anaheim Ducks general manager Brian Burke.

Adds Gretzky of their battles of Alberta, "He kept coming at you to get you off your game. He did a good job on me."

The only other player to wear number 0 was goaltender Paul Bibeault when he was backup with the Montreal Canadiens in 1942-43.

No. 0

Says:

1. **Neil Sheehy,** Hartford Whalers

2. **Paul Bibeault,** Montreal Canadiens

"He had Wayne Gretzky and Dave Semenko simultaneously and equally distraught. A shrewd negotiator even when he played."

Ron MacLean

Paul Bibeault

Neil Sheehy

Bet You Forgot

The No. 0 has been worn by two players in NHL history: Paul Bibeault and Neil Sheehy. Bibeault wore it while playing for the Montreal Canadiens as a backup goaltender during the 1942-43 season, but wore No. 1 later with the Canadiens, as well as Chicago, Boston, and Toronto. According to Canadiens historian Carl Lavigne, Bibeault must have been a confused man during that 1942–43 season as he wore three numbers: 0, 1, and 16. That season Bibeault appeared in all 50 games, playing 3,010 of a possible 3,060 minutes.

Prior to the 1998-99 season, the NHL ruled that neither 0 nor 00 could be worn any longer. It was believed it was because the league switched to a new computer software program for statistics, which tracked players by their sweater numbers and it could not recognize either 0 or 00. League officials today don't believe that to be the reason, but also can't track down through the minutes of league meetings why it happened.

Terry Sawchuk

Regarded as being one of the great money goaltenders of his time, Terry Sawchuk played 21 seasons, with stops in Detroit, Toronto, Boston, Los Angeles, and finally New York. He won the Stanley Cup four times, the Vezina Trophy four times, and was rookie of the year in three leagues (United States Hockey League with Omaha, American Hockey League with Indianapolis, and the National Hockey League with Detroit).

Sawchuk's 103 career shutouts are still a league record. Originally property of Boston, Sawchuk was traded to Detroit and made his NHL debut near the end of the 1949-50 season. He was later moved back to Boston, but after a stressful year with the Bruins in the mid-50s Sawchuk retired briefly. He was lured out of retirement the following season when he was traded back to the Red Wings for a young forward named Johnny Bucyk, who went on to greatness with the Bruins.

Sawchuk became property of the Maple Leafs in 1964 when he was left unprotected in the Intraleague Draft. He wore number 30 mostly in Toronto, including 1967 when they won the Stanley Cup, and wore 24 for one season.

Sawchuk, whose nickname was "The Uke" or "Ukey" for his Ukrainian heritage, left the game as the winningest goaltender in league history, with 447 victories, but that distinction now belongs to Patrick Roy, who has 551 regular-season wins.

Sawchuk, a native of Winnipeg, retired in 1970. That same year he died at the age of 40 of internal injuries suffered a month earlier in a playful scuffle with a teammate. He was inducted into the Hockey Hall of Fame in 1971 and his sweater was retired by the Red Wings on March 6, 1994.

PLANTE   HALL   PARENT
VEZINA   BOWER

Says:

"In my books, the best goalie of all time. You can never judge goaltenders, or any hockey players for that matter, from era to era, but I would have loved to see the likes of Terry Sawchuk playing today, to see what he could do with these shooters. He would find it tough at first of course because they're shooting harder, but he would figure it out because all the Red Wings will tell you, in practice, every time there was a little prize, Terry would be very upset if they even beat him once."

Bob Cole

No. 1

1. **Terry Sawchuk**, Detroit Red Wings
2. **Jacques Plante**, Montreal Canadiens
3. **Georges Vezina**, Montreal Canadiens
4. **Glenn Hall**, Chicago Blackhawks
5. **Johnny Bower**, Toronto Maple Leafs
6. **Bernie Parent**, Philadelphia Flyers
7. **Lorne 'Gump' Worsley**, Montreal Canadiens
8. **George Hainsworth**, Montreal Canadiens
9. **Walter 'Turk' Broda**, Toronto Maple Leafs
10. **Ed Giacomin**, New York Rangers

George Hainsworth

"Babe" Siebert

Bet You Forgot

This is a classic number for NHL goaltenders, having been worn by many of the game's greats. But no member of the Minnesota Wild will ever wear it. The number was retired immediately after the team joined the NHL in 2000 to honour the fans who had waited for NHL hockey to return to the state after the previous franchise, the North Stars, moved to Dallas in 1993. Meantime, at least three players who were not goaltenders have worn the No. 1. All played for the Montreal Canadiens. They were Marty Burke, in 1928-29, Herb Gardiner, from 1926-28, and Albert "Babe" Siebert from 1936-39.

Doug Harvey

Harvey was the preeminent and dominant defenceman of his era. Blessed with great speed and skill, the native of Montreal won the Norris Trophy as top defenceman seven times in an eight-year span and won the Stanley Cup six times with the Canadiens, including an incredible five straight from 1956-60, an accomplishment that never has and probably never will be matched.

His brilliant 20-year career began in 1947-48 and when it was over, beyond the Norris Trophies and championships, he had been named to the NHL all-star team 11 times, including 10 times on the First Team.

Harvey was respected not only for his ability to rush the puck, something that dramatically changed the game, but also for his ability to defend, to block shots, and work the point on the power play. In short, he did it all and did it all very well. He went on to become captain of the Canadiens after Maurice "Rocket" Richard retired in 1960. The following season he joined the New York Rangers as a player-coach, winning his final Norris Trophy in the 1961-62 season. After brief stints in the AHL and with Detroit, Harvey eventually wound up with the expansion St. Louis Blues.

Harvey played 20 NHL seasons, registering 88 goals and 540 points at a time when defencemen weren't big points producers.

He was also one of the first players to help organize the Players' Association, which many believe in part led to his being traded to the Rangers and the long delay before his sweater was retired by Montreal in 1985. He was elected to the Hockey Hall of Fame in 1973 and died on December 26, 1989. He had long fought alcoholism and had been diagnosed with bipolar disorder.

As for why he wore number two, according to Harvey's biography *Doug: The Doug Harvey Story*, by William Brown, it appears he simply inherited the number.

"The Canadiens had traded defenceman Frank Eddolls partly on the assumption that Harvey would be able to take his place," wrote Brown. "Harvey was given the number 2 that Eddolls had worn."

He made it considerably more famous.

Jacques Laperriere

No. 2

1. **Doug Harvey**, Montreal Canadiens
2. **Eddie Shore**, Boston Bruins
3. **Al MacInnis**, St. Louis Blues
4. **Viacheslav Fetisov**, New Jersey Devils
5. **Brad Park**, New York Rangers
6. **Tim Horton**, Buffalo Sabres
7. **Brian Leetch**, New York Rangers
8. **Jacques Laperriere**, Montreal Canadiens
9. **Red Horner**, Toronto Maple Leafs
10. **Carl Brewer**, Toronto Maple Leafs

Bet You Forgot

While Odie Cleghorn took care of the goals, older brother Sprague physically took care of opponents during the four seasons they played together for the Montreal Canadiens in the 1920s. Sprague was notorious for his temper and regularly punished opposing players who took liberties with his brother. Sadly, that closeness continued in death. Sprague died after being hit by a car in 1956, and on the day of his funeral, Odie died of heart failure. Reporters of the day speculated it was brought on by the stress of his brother's death.

Odie Cleghorn

Says:

"To this day, when people pick the all-time, all-star team for the NHL, one defenceman is Bobby Orr and the other is almost always Doug Harvey. He's in that category. He was probably the best all-around athlete that was ever produced in Montreal. He played pro football, pro baseball—I believe he led the league in hitting when he played pro baseball—he was quite a guy. He played with his head. Bobby Orr might have played a lot more from his legs than Doug did, but Harvey played with his head and he has six Stanley Cups.

Scott Stevens

When Scott Stevens threw a body check, he usually left a mark. A punishing—though clean—body checker, Stevens was an excellent stay-at-home defenceman and a great leader throughout his career. Drafted fifth overall in 1982 by the Washington Capitals, with whom he played nine seasons, he showed that he could also contribute offensively.

It was with the Capitals that he wore number three while making a name for himself on the blue line. "Three was what I wore in junior with the Kitchener Rangers," says Stevens. "They gave it to me in Washington and it was probably just because I wore it in junior, so I carried on with it and I was fine with that."

Stevens' career took a few odd twists as a result of the contract system in the NHL. In the summer of 1990 he signed with St. Louis as a restricted free agent, meaning the Capitals could either match the offer or receive compensation (five first-round draft picks). They took the latter and no doubt regretted it.

"When I got to St. Louis there weren't many good numbers left and 3 wasn't available because it had been taken out of circulation to honour Bob Gassoff, a defenceman who had died in a motorcycle accident," says Stevens. "Number 4 was taken, so they gave me the number 2."

He only wore it for a year. The following summer the Blues signed winger Brendan Shanahan as a restricted free agent from New Jersey, but an arbitrator ultimately ruled in favour of the Devils and awarded them Stevens as compensation. It didn't seem like a good idea at the time, but the move to the Devils was a great one for Stevens, who would become their captain and lead them to three Stanley Cup victories, all while reinforcing his reputation as a leader and crushing checker.

"In New Jersey, I really didn't have any say about what number I got," he says. "Lou [general manager Lamoriello] gave it to me. But 4 was a great number, so I wasn't complaining. A guy named Miles O'Connor had been wearing it, but he had been up and down to the minors, and Lou just took it away from him. Kenny (Daneyko), of course, had 3 and (Slava) Fetisov had 2, so they were out of the question."

Stevens retired in the fall of 2005 and his number 4 was retired in February 2006.

"I can't say I had a favourite number," he says. "I liked 2 and 3 but probably wound up liking 4 the best. I just like the look of the number and, of course, the great Bobby Orr had it. Growing up, the Maple Leafs were my team and I really like Borje Salming and the way he played. He blocked shots, was a good all-around player. I liked 3 in junior and at the start."

In the end, Stevens made them both famous.

No. 3

1. **Scott Stevens**, Washington Capitals
2. **Marcel Pronovost**, Detroit Red Wings
3. **Pierre Pilote**, Chicago Blackhawks
4. **Harry Howell**, New York Rangers
5. **J.C. Tremblay**, Montreal Canadiens
6. **Lionel Conacher**, Montreal Maroons
7. **James Patrick**, New York Rangers
8. **Emile Bouchard**, Montreal Canadiens
9. **Al Arbour**, Toronto Maple Leafs
10. **Ivan "Ching" Johnson**, New York Rangers

Pierre Pilote

Says:

"He was maybe the greatest open-ice hitter ever to play the game, no question about it. When he had that look in his eyes before the game you knew there would be trouble. I remember before that game, when he hit Lindros, I said Eric shouldn't be out there when a pit bull like Stevens is on the prowl."

Don Cherry

Marcel Pronovost

Bet You Forgot

Most hockey fans remember the late Fred Shero as being the coach of the Broad Street Bullies, the rough-and-tumble Philadelphia Flyers teams that won two Stanley Cups in the mid-1970s. But prior to that, Shero, one of the great minds of the game, wore No. 3 for the New York Rangers when he played defence for the Broadway Blueshirts in the 1940s.

Bobby Orr

"Number four, Bobby Orr."

It was heard often around rinks, but it sounded best coming from the PA announcer at the Boston Garden with his New England accent.

Orr is still arguably the greatest player—not just defenceman—ever to play in the NHL.

Like the legendary Doug Harvey before him, Orr was the dominant player of his era, and he changed how defencemen played the game. Indeed, Orr was brilliant at both ends of the rink. He had great speed, unbelievable skill, and was even surprisingly tough, although not always regarded for that part of his game.

The native of Parry Sound, Ontario, won the Norris Trophy as top defenceman in eight consecutive years, the Hart Trophy as most valuable player in the league three times, the Conn Smythe Trophy as most valuable player in the playoffs twice, and the Art Ross Trophy as regular-season scoring leader twice.

As a 14-year-old, the Boston Bruins, who owned his rights, had Orr playing junior with the Oshawa Generals. When he was 18, Orr was with the Bruins in the NHL. In his first game, against Detroit, he earned his first point and had a terrific game. He went on to win the Calder Trophy as top rookie and was a Second Team All-Star, finishing second in scoring amongst defencemen. Unfortunately, on one of his patented end-to-end rushes, Orr hurt his left knee that season. It was the start of many knee problems that would eventually abbreviate his career.

Orr became the first defenceman to score more than 40 goals (he had 46) in a season, and the first player to earn more than 100 (he had 102) assists in a season. Orr completely controlled games, changing speeds as he dashed up the ice, using his brilliant stickhandling ability to weave around players, often scoring highlight reel goals, including the Stanley Cup winner in 1970 against St. Louis, which has become a famous photo of number 4 flying through the air.

Orr's most productive season was 1970-71 when he registered a whopping 139 points and was a remarkable plus-124. He would later become the first player to sign a $1 million contract (five years at $200,000 per year). Sadly, though, troubles with his left knee (he had six operations by 1976) cut short Orr's career, forcing him to retire in 1978. The following year he was inducted into the Hockey Hall of Fame and is now a successful player agent.

When Orr first arrived in Boston, during his first pre-season, he wore number 27 in eight exhibition games, but later switched to 4 after, as the story goes, Junior Langlois didn't make the team. He was offered the chance to wear number 5, made famous by Dit Clapper, but declined and took 4, the closest available to 2, which is what Orr wore in junior in Oshawa. Number 2 was retired in Boston in honour of Eddie Shore.

"When I started the numbers were all assigned and we didn't care about the number, we just wanted the sweater," Orr says.

"In minor hockey I wore number two most of the time, just because that was a number defencemen wore. I wore two in junior with Oshawa because it was given to me.

"In camp with Boston I wore 27 most of the time, but I have a photo in which I was wearing 30 and I've seen a photo and it looks like I was wearing number one. But it was mostly 27, but before camp ended they switched me to number 4. A veteran defenceman, I believe it was Al Langlois, got hurt and they gave me his number.

"But nobody put a lot of thought into numbers, you just wanted to get that sweater and play in the NHL. I've heard stories about guys offering money to change numbers; that's outrageous. I even heard a story about a kid who went to Johnny Bucyk and asked if he could wear his number 9."

"What can I say? It's quite obvious No. 4 is my favourite number and Bobby is my favourite hockey player and the greatest player who ever lived or ever will live. Bobby Clarke said it best one time, when he said it's a shame there's not a higher league he could have gone to."

4

BELIVEAU STEVENS
KELLY GADSBY

Hap Day

Ron Francis

Bet You Forgot

Famed Carolina Hurricanes (née Hartford Whalers) centre and captain Ron Francis wore No. 4 during his first season with the Whalers in 1981-82. He switched to No. 10 the following season.

Vincent Lecavalier

No. 4

1. **Bobby Orr**, Boston Bruins
2. **Jean Beliveau**, Montreal Canadiens
3. **Red Kelly**, Toronto Maple Leafs
4. **Scott Stevens**, New Jersey Devils
5. **Bill Gadsby**, Detroit Red Wings
6. **Kevin Lowe**, Edmonton Oilers
7. **Mark Howe**, Detroit Red Wings
8. **Vincent Lecavalier**, Tampa Bay Lightning
9. **Rob Blake**, Los Angeles Kings
10. **Hap Day**, Toronto Maple Leafs

Bill Gadsby

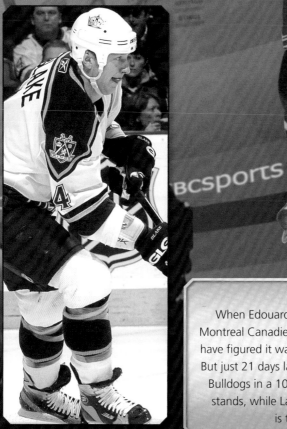

Rob Blake

Bet You Forgot

When Edouard "Newsy" Lalonde scored six goals for the Montreal Canadiens in a 14-7 rout of Toronto in 1920, he must have figured it was an NHL record that would stand for awhile. But just 21 days later, Joe Malone scored seven for the Quebec Bulldogs in a 10-7 victory over Toronto. Malone's record still stands, while Lalonde, who wore No. 4 for the Canadiens, is tied for second with six others.

Denis Potvin

Talk about pressure.

When he arrived in the NHL, drafted first overall in 1973, Denis Potvin had been labeled as the next Bobby Orr and was expected to take a sad-sack New York Islanders team and make it a winner.

Well, there is only one Orr, but Potvin did become a big-time star in the NHL. He won the Calder Trophy and went on to win the Norris Trophy—as top defenceman—three times. And he did eventually make champions of the Islanders, helping to lead them to four Stanley Cup victories in the 1980s.

A great skater, Potvin could also handle the puck well, had a terrific shot, and became noted for his punishing hip checks. Three times in his 15-season career he surpassed the 30-goal mark and one year earned 101 points, feats that few defencemen not named Orr could achieve. When he retired in 1988, Potvin actually had eclipsed Orr's goal-scoring and points record for defencemen.

"I wore number 2 when I first started in junior in Ottawa as a 14-year-old, then switched to 7," says Potvin, who was elected to the Hockey Hall of Fame in 1991. "I don't quite know why I made the switch, but it's just a number I liked. I liked single-digit numbers. That's the number I wanted with the Islanders.

"When I got to Peterborough for my first training camp with the Islanders the trainer, Jim Pickard, asked me what number I liked. I hadn't really watched the Islanders, so I said 7. I didn't realize a veteran player, Germain Gagnon, had 7.

"Being a 35, 36-year-old veteran, I guess he didn't like it, because the next morning, unbeknownst to me, a conversation took place with Jim Pickard about the number. Germain put a note up on my stall saying I could have number 7 for $500. I took the note to Jim Pickard and said, 'What's the next number available?' He said 5 and that was that. I felt embarrassed, but I didn't know and I didn't mean for Jim to ask.

"So I wore 5. There were certain numbers you would never wear: 3, 4, 9..."

There was talk that Potvin wore 5 for Leo Boivin, who taught him the hip check and coached him his final junior year in Ottawa.

"Leo certainly had a big influence on my career," says Potvin. "He was a great transition coach my last year and was very helpful. But I never realized and didn't until this day that he wore number 5."

The Islanders retired the number 5 on February 1, 1992, the first sweater raised to the rafters in franchise history.

GEOFFRION   CLAPPER   LANGWAY
LIDSTROM   LAPOINTE

Hockey Night Says:

"A hard-nosed defenceman and probably one of the toughest players of his time. When the Islanders won those Cups back in the 80s he was the reason why. Drafted No. 1 overall when the Islanders were dead last, he lifted that team and showed by example what they could do and they did it, and won four Stanley Cups."

Bob Cole

No. 5

1. **Denis Potvin**, New York Islanders
2. **Bernard Geoffrion**, Montreal Canadiens
3. **Nicklas Lidstrom**, Detroit Red Wings
4. **Dit Clapper**, Boston Bruins
5. **Guy Lapointe**, Montreal Canadiens
6. **Rod Langway**, Washington Capitals
7. **Bill Barilko**, Toronto Maple Leafs
8. **Rob Ramage**, St. Louis Blues
9. **Mike Ramsey**, Buffalo Sabres
10. **Max Bentley**, Chicago Blackhawks

Bet You Forgot

Early in his career, Montreal Canadiens winger Bernie Geoffrion told his wife that his number would one day hang from the rafters, an honour Marlene understood. She was the daughter of Canadiens legend Howie Morenz, whose No. 7 was the first number retired by the club following his death in 1937. But, like Morenz, Geoffrion did not live to see his sweater retired. Tragically, he succumbed to cancer on March 11, 2006, the same day his number was raised at the Bell Centre. Geoffrion, nicknamed "Boom Boom" for his slapshot, was the second player ever to score 50 goals in a season and won six Stanley Cups with the Canadiens from 1950-64.

Rod Langway

Bernie Geoffrion

Ace Bailey

Ace Bailey is the first NHL player to have his number retired, but he paid a heavy price for the honour.

A star left winger with the Toronto Maple Leafs from 1926-33, Bailey's career was ended when he was viciously checked by Boston defenceman Eddie Shore during a game in Boston on December 12, 1933. Bailey, born Irvine Wallace in Bracebridge, Ontario, in 1903, fell hard to the ice, banging his head so badly that it was originally feared he would not survive.

Boston police even considered pressing manslaughter charges against Shore, but Bailey pulled through and the case was dropped. Bailey, however, would never play hockey again, and the NHL quickly arranged an exhibition game for which the proceeds would go to the Leafs' player and his family. The teams would consist of Bailey's Leafs versus a squad consisting of players from all the other teams in the league, and it was the precursor to the NHL's All-Star Game, though it would be 13 years before it would become an annual event.

Prior to the Bailey benefit game at Maple Leaf Gardens on February 14, 1934, Leafs owner Conn Smythe took to the ice and announced that Bailey's number 6 would never be worn again by a Toronto Maple Leaf. That promise was only broken by Bailey himself when he asked a young Ron Ellis to wear his number 6 many years later.

However, since Ellis retired, Bailey's number 6 and Bill Barilko's number 5 are the only numbers no longer available to Maple Leafs players and were raised to rafters of Maple Leaf Gardens together on October 17, 1992. All subsequent numbers hanging from the roof of the Leafs' current arena, the Air Canada Centre, are only "honoured" and can be worn by current players.

Prior to his injury, Bailey was a key component of Smythe's Leafs, leading the league in goals with 22 and points with 32 in 44 games of the 1928-29 season.

He won one Stanley Cup with the Leafs, defeating the New York Rangers in the 1932 final.

Bailey was inducted into the Hockey Hall of Fame in 1975 and passed away in 1992 at the age of 88.

No. 6

1. **Ace Bailey**, Toronto Maple Leafs
2. **Phil Housley**, Buffalo Sabres
3. **Toe Blake**, Montreal Canadiens
4. **Fred "Bun" Cook**, New York Rangers
5. **Ron Ellis**, Toronto Maple Leafs
6. **Ken Morrow**, New York Islanders
7. **Jim Schoenfeld**, Buffalo Sabres
8. **Neil Colville**, New York Rangers
9. **Ralph Backstrom**, Montreal Canadiens
10. **Jimmy Roberts**, Montreal Canadiens

"Bun" Cook

Ron Ellis

Bet You Forgot

We don't think his sweater had polka dots or flowers, but No. 6 was the number worn by Don Cherry during his one and only NHL appearance. A career minor-league defenceman, Cherry was called up to the Boston Bruins during the 1955 playoffs. Cherry, of course, later achieved success first as an AHL, then NHL coach—winning coach of the year honours in both leagues—and after that as a star commentator on CBC's *Hockey Night in Canada*.

Howie Morenz

Canadiens star Howie Morenz, who was nicknamed "the Mitchell Meteor" (for his birthplace and great speed) and later "the Stratford Streak" (after his family moved), is the last player to wear number seven for Montreal.

Morenz died at the age of 34 of a blood clot, just weeks after he had broken his leg in a game against Chicago. The funeral, held on March 11, 1937, attracted thousands of mourners to the Forum to honour Morenz, who was voted Canada's greatest hockey player of the first half of the century.

According to *The Little Book of Hockey Sweaters*, when Morenz signed his first contract with Montreal on July 7, 1923, manager Leo Dandurand gave him the number 7. No other player wore it in Montreal after him, although Morenz wore it again when he was reacquired from Chicago late in his career.

Morenz won the Stanley Cup in his first season in Montreal and was part of two more championship teams. He also won the Hart Trophy three times and was considered one of the first true superstars of the game, scoring 271 goals in 14 seasons.

Interestingly, Morenz's daughter, Marlene, married Bernie Geoffrion, who would later become a star with the Canadiens. Geoffrion's number 5 was retired by the Habs on March 11, 2006 (the same day, 69 years later, of Morenz's funeral). During the ceremony, while Geoffrion's sweater was being raised in Bell Centre, Morenz's was lowered to meet it, then the two were raised together.

Morenz was one of the first inductees into the Hockey Hall of Fame in 1945.

"Don't forget that during the Depression in the Thirties, when hockey and everything else was at the low ebb economic-wise, they called Howie Morenz the Babe Ruth of hockey. He was the guy that the people paid to see, on both sides of the border, especially in the United States, so he was quite an influence on the game that way."

Dick Irvin

Bill Barber

No. 7

1. **Howie Morenz**, Montreal Canadiens
2. **Phil Esposito**, Boston Bruins
3. **Ted Lindsay**, Detroit Red Wings
4. **Paul Coffey**, Edmonton Oilers
5. **Ray Bourque**, Boston Bruins
6. **Rod Gilbert**, New York Rangers
7. **Tim Horton**, Toronto Maple Leafs
8. **Lanny McDonald**, Toronto Maple Leafs
9. **Bill Barber**, Philadelphia Flyers
10. **Rick Martin**, Buffalo Sabres

Phil Esposito

Ted Lindsay

Bet You Forgot

Seven is the number that has been retired the most, in honour
of nine players: Phil Esposito (Boston), Howie Morenz (Montreal),
Ted Lindsay (Detroit), Rod Gilbert (New York Rangers), Bill Barber
(Philadelphia), Rick Martin (Buffalo), Neal Broten (Dallas),
Paul Coffey (Edmonton), and Yvon Labre (Washington).

Cam Neely

Mention the name Cam Neely and you automatically think power forward.

That and a career that ended far too soon and saw far too many injuries.

But during his 10 seasons with the Boston Bruins, the big right winger from Comox, B.C. was something to behold. He was tough in the corners, could throw thundering checks, but also had a big shot and a deft scoring touch.

In junior, with the Portland Winter Hawks—who he helped lead to a Memorial Cup championship—Neely was a top scorer, which prompted the Vancouver Canucks to draft him ninth overall in 1983. Neely didn't put up big numbers in Vancouver in his three seasons with the Canucks, but he certainly did better after being traded to the Bruins along with a first-round pick for centre Barry Pederson.

At the time, the deal seemed like a good one for the Canucks. It turned out to be a great one for the Bruins.

Neely scored 36 goals his first season in Boston, then 42 the next, and three times scored 50 or more goals. Indeed, after returning from two severely shortened seasons because of thigh and knee injuries, Neely scored 50 goals in 49 games, and became third fastest to reach 50 goals in league history. In his final five seasons, Neely never played more than 49 games because of his injury problems.

He never won a Stanley Cup with the Bruins, but twice got them to the finals, losing both times to the Edmonton Oilers. Neely retired in 1996 at age 31 after 13 NHL seasons, having played just 726 games. He finished with 395 goals and 694 regular-season points. He was inducted into the Hockey Hall of Fame in 2005.

As for number 8, which the Bruins retired on January 12, 2004, it wasn't Neely's first choice.

"After I was traded it was the number given to me by the Bruins," explains Neely. "As a kid I wore number 12. Growing up in the Vancouver area, Stan Smyl was one of my favourite players. In junior, 12 wasn't available so I wore 21, which is what I wore in Vancouver.

"When I got traded to Boston, 21 was taken (by Frank Simonetti) and they gave me 8. The guy wearing 21 got sent to the minors a while later and I asked the trainer if I could have it. He said he would ask and get back to me. A few days later, the trainer said (Bruins general manager) Harry Sinden likes you in 8 and that was that."

No. 8

1. **Cam Neely**, Boston Bruins
2. **Teemu Selanne**, Anaheim Ducks
3. **Igor Larionov**, Detroit Red Wings
4. **Larry Murphy**, Washington Capitals
5. **Barclay Plager**, St. Louis Blues
6. **Ken Hodge**, Boston Bruins
7. **Mark Recchi**, Pittsburgh Penguins
8. **Dick Duff**, Montreal Canadiens
9. **Randy Carlyle**, Winnipeg Jets
10. **Alex Ovechkin**, Washington Capitals

Alex Ovechkin

Teemu Selanne

Says:

"The ultimate power forward is Cam Neely. This guy could do it all. He could fight, hit, block shots, and still get 50 goals. It's a crying shame Ulf Samuelsson ended his career early. Cam was just great."

Don Cherry

Bet You Forgot

In honour of his mother, Tatania, Washington Capitals youngster Alexander Ovechkin wears No. 8. Tatania was a member of the Soviet Union's Olympic women's basketball team, which won gold medals in both 1976 and 1980. She wore number 8.

9

Gordie Howe

"Mr. Hockey," as the legendary Hall of Fame right winger Gordie Howe is known, played 26 seasons in the NHL and an additional six seasons in the WHA. He was both a gifted goal scorer and a great playmaker, but he was also tough, noted for his famous elbows and great strength. Indeed, the term "the Gordie Howe Hat Trick" soon became part of the lexicon of hockey, signifying a goal, an assist, and a fight all in one game.

When Howe arrived in Detroit, he first wore sweater number 17 as an 18-year-old rookie in 1946-47. Prior to the beginning of his second season, the Red Wings traded Roy Conacher, who was wearing number 9, to Chicago. Howe was offered the lower number, but was reluctant to make a switch. However, Red Wings trainer Lefty Wilson managed to convince him to change when he reminded Howe that the lower number meant a better berth on the trains.

His Red Wings number 9 became the favourite of Wayne Gretzky, who honoured his hero by wearing the twin nines. It is also worn by the character Cameron Frye in the movie *Ferris Bueller's Day Off*. And his number was retired by Detroit, Hartford, and Houston.

Incredibly, over his career Howe finished in the top five in scoring for 20 straight seasons. He led the Red Wings to four Stanley Cup victories and first place in the regular season for seven straight seasons between 1949 and 1956, a record that still stands.

With linemates Sid Abel, who actually wore number 9 for one season, and Ted Lindsay, they were known as The Production Line. Howe played pro hockey until he was 51 years old, playing all 80 games of his final season (1979-80), scoring 15 goals and accumulating 41 points. Howe stands third in NHL scoring with 1,850 points, including 801 goals.

Says:

"...e would be the most complete player of any I've
...n play the game. Shooting, stickhandling, skating,
...ghness, spirit—you name it, Gordie Howe was a
competitor in every sense of the word."

Bob Cole

9

RICHARD BATHGATE
HULL   MODANO

Bobby Hull

Bet You Forgot

For five games in the 2005-06 season, the final games of his career, Brett Hull was able to honour his father, Bobby, when he wore No. 9 with the Phoenix Coyotes. The number had actually been retired to honour Bobby's career with the Coyotes' predecessor, the Winnipeg Jets, back in 1989, but Brett was able to get permission from his dad to wear it. The Hulls are the only father-son

Maurice Richard

Mike Modano

No. 9

1. **Gordie Howe**, Detroit Red Wings
2. **Maurice Richard**, Montreal Canadiens
3. **Bobby Hull**, Chicago Blackhawks
4. **Andy Bathgate**, New York Rangers
5. **Mike Modano**, Dallas Stars
6. **Ted Kennedy**, Toronto Maple Leafs
7. **John Bucyk**, Boston Bruins
8. **Lanny McDonald**, Calgary Flames
9. **Charlie Conacher**, Toronto Maple Leafs
10. **Glenn Anderson**, Edmonton Oilers

Darryl Sittler

CBC

Bet You Forgot

After being traded from Toronto to Philadelphia during the 1981-82 season, Darryl Sittler wore No. 9 because veteran Reggie Leach wore Sittler's No. 27. When Leach signed with Detroit in the off-season, Sittler reclaimed No. 27.

10 Guy Lafleur

What the legendary Rocket Richard was to one generation of young French Canadian kids, Jean Beliveau was to another. And Guy Lafleur became to still another.

"When I was a kid, everyone wanted to be Beliveau," says Lafleur, who grew up in rural Thurso, Quebec, and became a Montreal Canadiens legend himself. "I only ever wore two numbers, 4 for Beliveau and number 10.

"The only time that I wore number 10 was in junior B. All the other years it was number 4. When I went to Montreal, number 10 was available."

Interestingly, when Lafleur went to Montreal, the first pick overall in 1971, he was figuratively passed the torch by Beliveau who had just retired. Lafleur had the opportunity to wear the hallowed number 4 but declined, understanding the overwhelming pressure it would have put on him—not that he wasn't already under pressure.

Canadiens general manager Sam Pollock worked his magic to get his team the first pick from the California Golden Seals to select Lafleur, who had starred with the Quebec Remparts. Had the Canadiens not gotten the pick, or not used it to pick him, Lafleur admitted later he would have signed with Quebec of the old World Hockey Association.

Lafleur spent 14 seasons with the Canadiens, winning the Stanley Cup five times before retiring just 19 games into the 1984-85 season at age 33. He retired for three years, but returned to play one season with the New York Rangers and two with the Nordiques.

The lasting image of Lafleur, who was known as "The Flower" (a literal translation of his surname), was of the fleet winger streaking down the right side, his hair flowing in the breeze, and unloading a big slapshot from the top of the faceoff circle.

Over his illustrious career, which took three years to really take flight and was dotted by some controversy off the ice, Lafleur scored 50 goals and 100 points in six consecutive seasons, the first player ever to accomplish that feat. He was the NHL scoring leader three times, won the Hart Trophy twice, and the Conn Smythe Trophy once. His 1,246 points are the most in Canadiens' history. He was one of just eight players ever to win the Stanley Cup, the scoring title, and most valuable player in the same season.

Lafleur, who was the sixth Canadien to have his sweater retired, was elected to the Hockey Hall of Fame in 1988 and became just the third player ever to resume his career after his induction.

Says:

"He was the most exciting player outside of Bobby Orr. He killed me many times, but he was a class act. He used to get ready like Bobby did, at the rink at 2:30 in the afternoon, pacing like a lion. Outside of Bobby Orr, I liked watching him the best. He was poetry on ice and a class guy. To see him going down the ice, that sweater rippling the breeze, his hair flowing—it was a picture to behold."

Don Cherry

10

HAWERCHUK RATELLE ARMSTRONG DELVECCHIO

Alex Delvecchio

Frank Mahovlich

Bet You Forgot

A trade can be an unsettling experience for players as they are forced to adjust to a new city, new teammates, and often wear a new number. Frank Mahovlich had to lose his No. 27 and instead wear No. 10 when he was traded from Detroit to Montreal in the 1970-71 season. However, he soon reacquired his No. 27 and the following season a rookie named Guy Lafleur made No. 10 his own.

No. 10

Pavel Bure

1. **Guy Lafleur**, Montreal Canadiens
2. **Dale Hawerchuk**, Winnipeg Jets
3. **George Armstrong**, Toronto Maple Leafs
4. **Jean Ratelle**, Boston Bruins
5. **Alex Delvecchio**, Detroit Red Wings
6. **Ron Francis**, Hartford Whalers
7. **Syl Apps**, Toronto Maple Leafs
8. **Pavel Bure**, Vancouver Canucks
9. **Tom Johnson**, Montreal Canadiens
10. **Gary Roberts**, Calgary Flames

11 Mark Messier

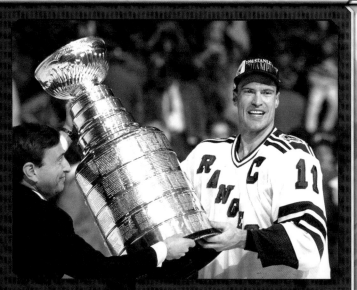

"Mark Messier is the greatest leader in the history of hockey."

Kevin Lowe, a former teammate, went on to suggest Messier may have also been the greatest leader in all of sports.

There is no denying Messier was a great leader, with an ability to inspire teammates either through fear or shared passion. He was a player who led by example, who had a win-at-all costs attitude and win he did. Often.

Indeed, leadership and the number 11 have been a part of the Messier family for many years.

Messier won the Stanley Cup six times, including four times in Edmonton playing with Wayne Gretzky. He went on to win for a fifth time in Edmonton after Gretzky had been traded to Los Angeles and he won his final Cup in New York, leading the Rangers to their first championship in 54 years, in a seven-game victory over the Vancouver Canucks in 1994.

Earlier that spring, there was Messier's famous guaranteed win in Game 6 of the Eastern Conference final against the New Jersey Devils. All he did that night was score three goals to lead his team to victory and avoid elimination. He went on to score the Cup-winning goal against the Canucks, becoming the only captain to lead two different teams to victory.

Messier was a force as a player. He had size and great strength, great speed, and wonderful hands. He could do it all; he could win with finesse or brute force, but always, with fierce determination.

He finished his 25-year career second all-time with 1,887 points; seventh all-time with 694 goals and third all-time with 1,193 assists. He has the record for most combined regular season and playoff games at 1,992. He won the Hart and Lester B. Pearson trophies twice, the Conn Smythe once.

On January 12, 2006 the Rangers retired his number 11. The Oilers did the same on February 27, 2007.

"I wore number 11 in honour of my dad, Doug," says Messier. "He wore the number when he was playing. I've worn that number for as long as I can remember, although in my first year in the World Hockey Association I was given 27 in Cincinnati. And I once wore 15 on a peewee team many, many years ago."

Doug Messier was a minor professional player for 10 years, most notably with the Portland Buckaroos of the Western Hockey League, where he wore number 11 for seven seasons.

PERREAULT GARTNER HADFIELD SHANAHAN SUTTER

Says:

"I'm not saying anything we don't all know, but he was an absolute great leader. He took over that New York Rangers club when they were on their way down, guaranteed a win, and then did the job. He was the meanest of them all. He would do whatever it took to win."

Don Cherry

No. 11

1. **Mark Messier**, Edmonton Oilers
2. **Gilbert Perreault**, Buffalo Sabres
3. **Brendan Shanahan**, New Jersey Devils
4. **Mike Gartner**, Washington Capitals
5. **Brian Sutter**, St. Louis Blues
6. **Vic Hadfield**, New York Rangers
7. **Daniel Alfredsson**, Ottawa Senators
8. **Saku Koivu**, Montreal Canadiens
9. **Busher Jackson**, Toronto Maple Leafs
10. **Howie Meeker**, Toronto Maple Leafs

Bet You Forgot

Gilbert Perreault, centre of the famed French Connection line, has an interesting tale to tell about how he got his number and first NHL team. In the 1970 entry draft, the first pick was determined by the spin of a ceremonial roulette wheel. Buffalo Sabres general manager Punch Imlach won a coin flip and chose his favourite number, 11, for the spin. When the wheel stopped, NHL president Clarence Campbell announced it had stopped on the number one, which meant the Vancouver Canucks would have received the first pick. But, according to the Hockey Hall of Fame, Imlach examined the wheel and noticed it had stopped on number 11. Perreault was selected by the Sabres and wore No. 11 his entire career. Perreault

Gilbert Perreault

Dickie Moore

Dickie Moore has a lot of fond memories of wearing his Montreal Canadiens sweater and the number 12. He even has one from the night someone else wore the sweater.

"In his first tryout game with Montreal, Jean Beliveau was given my sweater, number 12," recalls Moore. "And he went out that night and scored three goals. This was when he came up from Quebec. I thought I better make sure I play well the next game."

As it turned out, when Beliveau came up to the Canadiens for good, he was given a selection of numbers from which to choose, and 12 wasn't among them. He decided on No. 4, especially because his favoured number 9 was still being occupied by Rocket Richard. The same goes for Moore.

"In junior, I wore 11 then 9 because of the Rocket," said Moore. "All the kids seemed to want to wear that number. When I got to the Canadiens, Dick Irvin Sr. handed me the number 12 and said, 'Do you think you're tough enough to wear it?' And that was it. Murph Chamberlain wore it a few years earlier, but I don't know how tough he was."

Moore played 14 seasons in the NHL and won the Stanley Cup six times, including five in a row with Montreal, a record many believe will never be broken. He scored 20 more goals in six different seasons and won the scoring title twice, in 1958 and 1959. His 96 points in 1958-59 broke the pre-expansion league record set by Gordie Howe.

The Canadiens retired his number 12 prior to a game against Toronto on November 12, 2005. They also honoured Yvan Cournoyer, who inherited the number from Moore in 1963.

"Yvan carried the torch so high, he brought it even higher than I did," Moore said.

After Cournoyer, who won four straight Cups from 1976-79, Mike Keane and Darcy Tucker also wore the number 12.

"I was proud to watch guys wear my number," Moore said. "Mike Keane wore it with so much pride that it made me even prouder."

No. 12

1. **Dickie Moore**, Montreal Canadiens
2. **Yvan Cournoyer**, Montreal Canadiens
3. **Sid Abel**, Detroit Red Wings
4. **Jarome Iginla**, Calgary Flames
5. **Adam Oates**, Boston Bruins
6. **Wayne Cashman**, Boston Bruins
8. **Gord Drillon**, Toronto Maple Leafs
9. **Adam Graves**, Edmonton Oilers
10. **Pat Stapleton**, Chicago Blackhawks

Says:

"Dickie Moore is one of the great competitors of all time. He won the scoring title with 96 points and played the last six weeks with a broken wrist. The doctor told him he shouldn't play, but he said he could—and did—and hung on to win the scoring. One of the toughest guys I've watched play that had the skill he's got, and his competitive edges were unparalleled on those skilled Montreal teams. They needed a little grit and they got a lot of it from Dickie Moore."

Harry Neale

Bet You Forgot

Considered hockey's first superstar, Howie Morenz led the Montreal Canadiens for 11 seasons in the 1920s and 30s. But even the greatest go into decline, and when injuries began to slow up Morenz he was traded, first to Chicago and then the New York Rangers. It was in New York that Morenz wore No. 12 instead of his usual No. 7, but it was only for 19 games in the 1935-36 season. The following season—his last in the NHL—he returned to Montreal and he finished his career with his familiar number on his back.

Sid Abel

Yvan Cournoyer

Mats Sundin

So much for superstition.

According to Sundin, "In Europe, number 13 isn't bad luck. In Europe, eight is considered unlucky."

As a kid, Sundin wore 13 because it signified his birthday, February 13, 1971. He also liked the number 19, but when he got to Quebec chose 13.

"In Quebec," he says, "the number 19 (Joe Sakic) wasn't an option."

And the rest, as they say, is history.

Sundin, the first European to be selected first overall in the NHL draft in 1989 by the Quebec Nordiques, carved out quite a career for himself. He was the first Swedish-born player to reach 500 career goals (and enters the 2007-08 season with 523) and 1,000 points (he has 1,243), the most ever by a Swede. He also holds the current NHL record with 15 overtime goals, which would explain why his nickname back home, according to Swedish journalists, is "Sudden."

Sundin was acquired by the Maple Leafs in the summer of 1994 in a blockbuster deal that involved fan favourite Wendel Clark heading to Quebec, but Sundin quickly endeared himself to the Toronto fans. He became the 16th captain in club history in 1997 and entered the 2007-08 season just one goal behind Darryl Sittler for the club record with 389 and seven points shy of the all-time team points record of 916.

Over his career, Sundin has used his size and strength to become a consistent point producer with the Leafs. He helped lead Sweden to a gold medal in the 2006 Winter Olympics.

Ken Linseman

No. 13

1. **Mats Sundin**, Toronto Maple Leafs
2. **Teemu Selanne**, Winnipeg Jets
3. **Pavel Datsyuk**, Detroit Red Wings
4. **Ken Linseman**, Boston Bruins
5. **Ray Whitney**, Carolina Hurricanes
6. **Vyacheslav Kozlov**, Detroit Red Wings
7. **Valeri Kamensky**, Quebec Nordiques/Colorado Avalanche
8. **Bill Guerin**, Boston Bruins
9. **Alexei Zhamnov**, Chicago Blackhawks
10. **Dave Christian**, Winnipeg Jets

Bet You Forgot

Considering it is one of the lower numbers, not many players have opted for No. 13 in comparison with so many others, but that's likely because hockey players can be a superstitious lot. The first player to wear No. 13 was Lorenzo Bertrand, who wore it for one game with Montreal in the 1910-11 season of the National Hockey Association. Two teams—New Jersey and Minnesota—have never had a player wear the number.

Teemu Selanne

Says:

"*Mats Sundin gets a lot of criticism in Toronto for reasons I don't know other than the fact they haven't won a Stanley Cup with him there. He's the fitness king of the Maple Leafs and I think he's one of the great players to have ever worn the Toronto Maple Leafs uniform. He's big, he's strong, he plays with a little burr under his saddle on occasion, and if he had had the wingers that some of the other high-scoring centres in the National Hockey League have had, his point total would be even better.*"

14

Dave Keon

Dave Keon will be remembered as being one of the greatest Toronto Maple Leafs of all time.

A fast, yet elegant, skater, Keon was a gifted playmaker and a good goal scorer, and made 14 the number thousands of kids across the country wanted to wear. Interestingly, it was not a number Keon wanted to wear himself at first.

"I wore 9 when I was playing junior B and junior A with St. Mike's," says Keon, who knew he wasn't going to get that number in Toronto because it belonged to Dick Duff. "In my first training camp they gave me number 8, then 24, then they gave me 14. But I didn't want it.

"It had not been a very successful number, meaning it was a number they would give to a guy who was called up from Rochester [the minors]. But I had to wear it, it was the number I was given, and I wound up keeping it the rest of the way."

Indeed, Keon wore it through his 15 seasons with the Leafs, then with Minnesota, New England, and Indianapolis of the World Hockey Association, and finally with Hartford back in the NHL before retiring in 1982.

After a successful junior career at St. Michael's College, Keon joined the Leafs in 1960 and his 20 goals and 45 points earned him the Calder Trophy. He went on to score 20 goals a season for five more consecutive seasons and 11 times overall in Toronto. Three times he led the Leafs in scoring, and twice he won the Lady Byng Trophy.

As good as he was offensively, with a backhand shot like no other, Keon was also a great defensive player, a terrific penalty killer, and was credited with shutting down Montreal's top scorers when the Leafs won their last Stanley Cup in 1967, when he won the Conn Smythe Trophy.

In total, he won the Stanley Cup four times during the 1960s in Toronto and was captain for six seasons, before a messy battle with owner Harold Ballard led to his departure to the WHA and an estrangement from the organization that didn't really end until 2007.

But years after Keon had left the organization, number 14 has still remained a fan favourite.

"If they had given me a choice of numbers," says Keon, "I would have picked 15. That's what I wore as a kid for my cousin (former Leaf) Tod Sloan. Either that or number 11 (Sloan also wore 11), I liked that number for some reason. But 14 turned out to be pretty good."

Keon was inducted into the Hockey Hall of Fame in 1986.

Says:

"He's the best two-way player in Maple Leafs history in my opinion. His goals and points are flattering when you think his job was to play against the opposing team's best centre almost shift for shift. And we're talking about Beliveau, Delvecchio, Mikita, and the great centres of the game, yet Dave was right up there among the highest-scoring Leafs. He was defensively terrific and took great pride making things miserable, if not physically, then mentally, for the players who played against him. He's the only guy I know who had a backhand slapshot and he scored a lot of goals with it."

Harry Neale

No. 14

1. **Dave Keon**, Toronto Maple Leafs
2. **Brendan Shanahan**, Detroit Red Wings
3. **Theoren Fleury**, Calgary Flames
4. **Kent Nilsson**, Calgary Flames
5. **Dave Andreychuk**, Toronto Maple Leafs
6. **Claude Provost**, Montreal Canadiens
7. **Mario Tremblay**, Montreal Canadiens
8. **Craig MacTavish**, Edmonton Oilers
9. **Rene Robert**, Buffalo Sabres
10. **Bob Bourne**, New York Islanders

Theoren Fluery

Brendan Shanahan

Brendan Shanahan

Apparently, Brendan Shanahan is not a sentimental guy. The rugged winger said he's never really had an attachment to any number and when he was traded from Hartford to Detroit in 1996, Red Wings coach Scotty Bowman asked him what number he wanted. Shanahan simply replied: "What numbers are available?" Told 12 or 14, he took 14. "Other than the Rangers," Shanahan said, "I've changed my number every team I've gone to."

Milt Schmidt

Milt Schmidt was invited to the Boston Bruins training camp back in 1935 for a tryout, but the 17-year-old so impressed coach Art Ross he was offered a contract.

"I turned it down," recalls Schmidt. "They offered me $2,000."

Schmidt did eventually sign with the Bruins that fall, and after a stint in the minors with Providence went on to greatness in Boston, starting in 1937, playing on the famed Kraut Line with childhood friends Woody Dumart and Bobby Bauer.

In 1939-40, that line finished first, second, and third in league scoring, the first time in league history that had happened.

A determined, hard-working centre, Schmidt was noted for his playmaking skills during his 16-season career, which was interrupted by a stint in the Air Force in World War II.

He won the Stanley Cup with the Bruins in 1939 and 1941. He led the league in scoring in 1940 and won the Hart Trophy in 1951. Schmidt retired in 1954-55 season because of bad knees with 229 goals and 575 points. At the time, he was third in career points in the NHL. After retiring, he went on to coach and manage the Bruins and was general manager in Washington.

As for the number 15...

"There is no story to it whatsover, it's the number they gave me when I first was brought up and I was just pleased to be a professional hockey player and to be playing with the likes of Eddie Shore and Dit Clapper," said Schmidt. "There weren't many professional players in those days in the NHL and it was an honour to be one.

"I wore 14 for Providence in the minors in 1936, which is the number they gave me. Then they gave me 15 in Boston. I was happy to have worn 15 for my career and I am very proud they retired the number.

"After they retired my number (March 13, 1980) the manager at the time, Harry Sinden, asked me if they could take it down. He said the numbers were getting so high they were looking like a football team. I said, hey, if you want to do it, what can I do? Maybe there would be some criticism, but it's up to you."

The number remained retired. Schmidt was inducted into the Hockey Hall of Fame in 1961.

No. 15

1. **Milt Schmidt**, Boston Bruins
2. **Bobby Smith**, Montreal Canadiens
3. **Dany Heatley**, Ottawa Senators
4. **John MacLean**, New Jersey Devils
5. **Bert Olmstead**, Montreal Canadiens
6. **Bobby Rousseau**, Montreal Canadiens
7. **Anders Hedberg**, New York Rangers
8. **Rejean Houle**, Montreal Canadiens
9. **Bill Harris**, Toronto Maple Leafs
10. **Dave Gagner**, Minnesota North Stars

Says:

"I saw Milt Schmidt only near the tail end of his career and to this day I think he's one of the greatest hockey players I ever saw. I can still see Milt coming down the ice, wearing his No. 15, playing the Canadiens and splitting the defence. You don't see that very often anymore, where a guy tore right through the two defencemen. He was a tough hockey player. It's strange, in those days, some of the best hockey players were the toughest hockey players. They led the league, were the all-stars, and boy, Milt Schmidt was as tough as you could get. I always consider him all-around. There are some guys who are good offence, or good defence, but Milt Schmidt.... I know my father had a great admiration for that whole Kraut Line, including Milt Schmidt, of course."

Dick Irvin

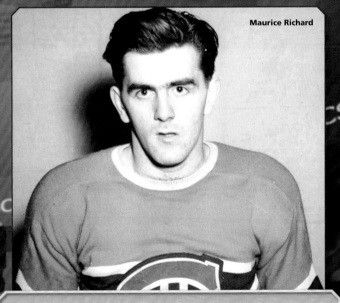

Maurice Richard

Bet You Forgot

When Maurice "Rocket" Richard broke into the NHL with the Montreal Canadiens in the 1942-43 season, he wore No. 15 and thought nothing of it. He switched to his more famous No. 9 after suffering a string of injuries and bad luck. He asked Canadiens coach Dick Irvin if he could change. After the birth of his daughter, Huguette, in 1943, who happened to weigh in at nine pounds when she arrived, he chose No. 9.

16

Henri Richard

Henri Richard is a winner. Plain and simple.

Incredibly, the Pocket Rocket, as he is known, in reference to being the younger brother of Maurice "The Rocket" Richard, won the Stanley Cup a record 11 times and played in 12 final series.

He shares the record, with Red Kelly, for having played the most games (65) in the Stanley Cup finals, totaling 47 points. Richard was the ninth player to reach 1,000 career points, was a first team all-star once and a second team all-star three times. In 1,256 regular-season games, he scored 358 goals and earned 1,046 points, as well as 129 additional points in 180 playoff games.

Though he was just 5-foot-7 and 160 pounds, Richard was not afraid to battle for pucks. An elegant skater, he was a great playmaker but also a good scorer. Despite his remarkable accomplishment of winning the Cup 11 times, including five straight, in many ways Richard did and continues to live in the shadow of his famous brother and other Canadiens greats such as Jean Beliveau.

Like most kids growing up in Quebec, he had an affinity for the number 9 worn by his brother.

"In junior, I wore number 9," says Richard. "When I got to Montreal, of course, Maurice was still there so they gave me 16. Elmer Lach had left and I got his number. It was nice because Elmer coached me one year in junior."

Says:

"Henri Richard played in the shadow of his brother [Maurice Richard] or else his superstardom would have been even greater. Nobody will ever reach his 11 Stanley Cups— five in his first five years in the league— and he's one of the all-time greats. He was a great skater and could really handle the puck and make plays. He may have been the fastest player I've seen with the puck. I don't know if he's the fastest player without it, but a lot of players slow down when they've got the puck— but he didn't, he sped up."

Harry Neale

CLARKE HULL GOULET DIONNE LAFONTAINE

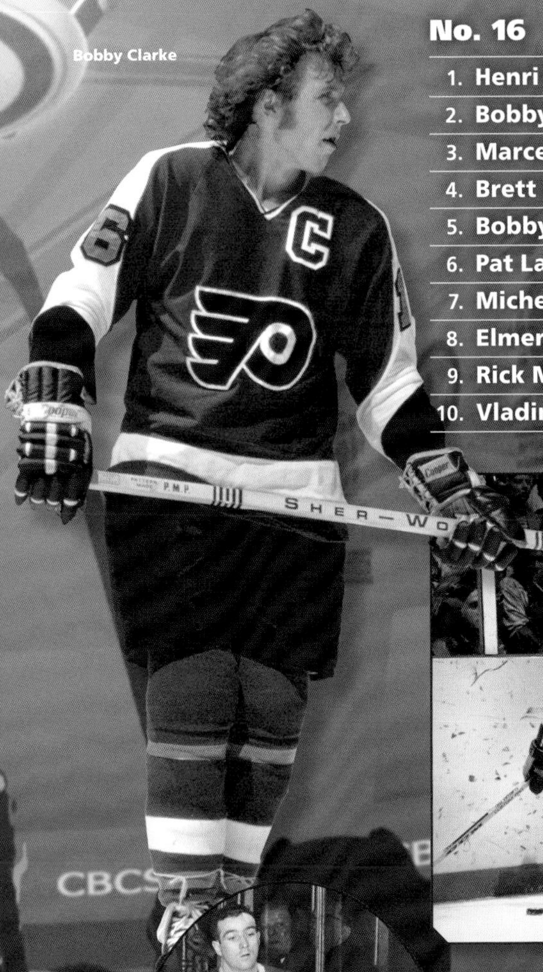

Bobby Clarke

No. 16

1. **Henri Richard**, Montreal Canadiens
2. **Bobby Clarke**, Philadelphia Flyers
3. **Marcel Dionne**, Los Angeles Kings
4. **Brett Hull**, St. Louis Blues
5. **Bobby Hull**, Chicago Blackhawks
6. **Pat LaFontaine**, New York Islanders
7. **Michel Goulet**, Chicago Blackhawks
8. **Elmer Lach**, Montreal Canadiens
9. **Rick Middleton**, Boston Bruins
10. **Vladimir Konstantinov**, Detroit Red Wings

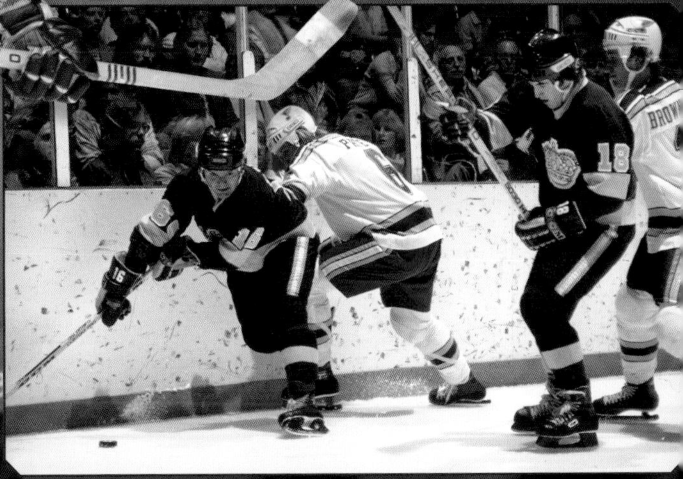

Marcel Dionne

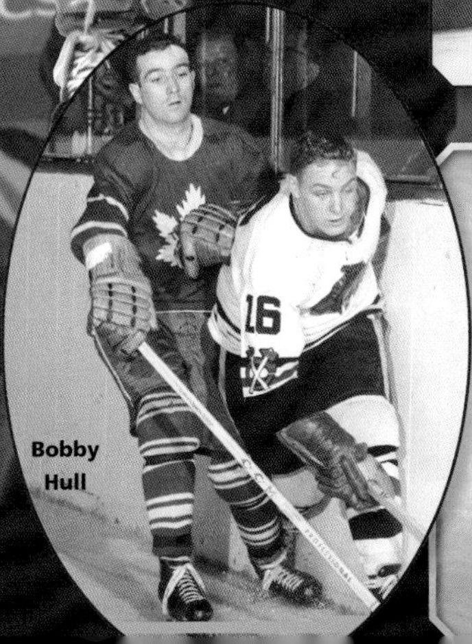

Bobby Hull

Bet You Forgot

This is the first and last number Bobby Hull wore in the NHL. From 1957 to 1962, the great left winger wore No. 16 for the Chicago Blackhawks and even wore No. 7 before settling on No. 9. But after a sojourn with the Winnipeg Jets in the rival World Hockey Association, Hull found himself again in the NHL with the Hartford Whalers. Alas, No. 9 was taken by none other than Gordie Howe, so Hull again wore No. 16 for the nine games he played in the 1979-80 season.

17

Jari Kurri

Jari Kurri admits he watched history unfold from one of the best vantage points—right beside Wayne Gretzky.

Indeed, Kurri and Gretzky formed a dynamic partnership with the Edmonton Oilers, winning the Stanley Cup together on the Oilers' dynasty teams four times. Kurri, one of the top right wingers to play the game, went on with Mark Messier to win it for a fifth time after Gretzky had moved on.

But Kurri was a big part of the glory years. He scored 40 or more goals in seven straight seasons, including a career-high 71 (then a record for right wingers) in 1984-85 (135 points), followed by 68 goals the next season. As great as he was scoring goals and helping to set up Gretzky and company, Kurri was also regarded as being one of the top defensive forwards in the game.

Drafted 69th overall in 1980, Kurri had played three seasons with Jokerit in the Finnish league, where he wore number 11. He stepped in and made an immediate impact with the Oilers, averaging a point a game in his first season.

"They gave me number 17 when I came to Edmonton," says Kurri, who is now the general manager of the Finnish national team. "I had worn it with the national team, so maybe that's what they were thinking. But I didn't ask for it. I had worn 11 with my club team and Mess [Mark Messier] had that in Edmonton obviously, so maybe that's why they leaned to 17."

Kurri wound up wearing 17 throughout his illustrious career, which involved moving on to Los Angeles to join Gretzky for four seasons, then moves to the New York Rangers, Anaheim, and Colorado before he retired in 1998 as the highest-scoring European with 601 goals and 1,398 points. He was a money player as well, having great success in the playoffs. During the 1985 playoffs, he tied a league record with 19 goals.

He was inducted into the Hockey Hall of Fame in 2001, the first Finn to be so honoured, and his number 17 was retired by the Oilers on October 6, 2001, as well as by the Finnish national team.

"I never had a favourite number," says Kurri. "I wore 16 before I wore 11, then I got 17. When I was kid, when I was nine years old, I wore number 9 playing for a team called the Toronto Maple Leafs."

CLARK HULL KOVALCHUK
BRIND'AMOUR REARDON

Says:

"I really respected him before, but it wasn't until I had the opportunity to play on the same team that I fully appreciated how good he was defensively. And he was one of the guys that I felt was actually aiming with a one-timer. Most guys just try to put it on the net but I think Jari had the ability to aim his one-timer."

Kelly Hrudey

Bet You Forgot
Number choice isn't easy. Just ask Brett Hull. "Everybody thought I wore number 16 for my father, but that wasn't the case. In Calgary, I wanted 15 because that's what my brother Blake wore. I thought it would be cool, but Robin Bartell had 15 so I took 16. It was close. In Dallas, Pat Verbeek had 16 so I had to chose from 27 and 22. I just took 22, it was the best available. In Detroit, 16 was out of commission for Vladimir Konstantinov and my options were limited, so I took 17. It's close."

No. 17

1. **Jari Kurri**, Edmonton Oilers
2. **Wendel Clark**, Toronto Maple Leafs
3. **Rod Brind'Amour**, Carolina Hurricanes
4. **Brett Hull**, Detroit Red Wings
5. **Ken Reardon**, Montreal Canadiens
6. **Ilya Kovalchuk**, Atlanta Thrashers
7. **Bobby Bauer**, Boston Bruins
8. **Mike Foligno**, Buffalo Sabres
9. **John LeClair**, Montreal Canadiens
10. **Ken Wharram**, Chicago Blackhawks

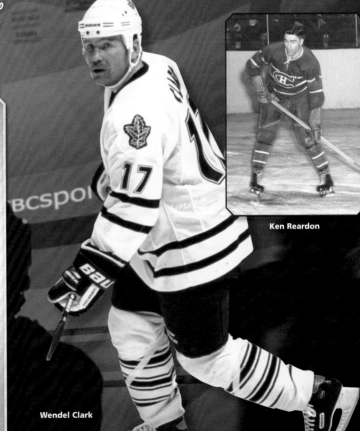

Ken Reardon

Wendel Clark

18 Denis Savard

Denis Savard was one of the most exciting players to ever play the game.

He was fast, a great puckhandler, elusive; Savard was a highlight reel. He could take the puck and, with his great speed, circle around the opposition's end before either darting in to make a play, or a pass, or score himself.

The late Danny Gallivan, a broadcast legend in Canada, used to refer to former Montreal Canadiens defenceman Serge Savard's (no relation) spins while carrying the puck as Savardian spinoramas. The same applied to Denis. Ironically, both wore number 18.

Savard was taken in the first round, third overall by the Blackhawks in 1980, from the Montreal Junior Canadiens. That year the NHL Canadiens had the number one pick overall and selected Doug Wickenheiser, who wasn't a popular choice in the province of Quebec. Wickenheiser never lived up to expectations and eventually was moved to St. Louis, where he sadly succumbed to cancer far too young.

Savard, meanwhile, had a tremendous career.

"When I got to Chicago the trainer, Lou Varga, said to me, 'I've got a number for you and we're going to make it good for you,'" says Savard. "It was number 18, which worked out because my cousin, Jean, was playing for the Quebec Remparts and he wore 18. So it was nice. In junior I wore 15 and 23, but I didn't have a favourite number. To me, the crests I wore on the front were more important than the number on the back."

After 10 seasons in Chicago, during which he five times surpassed 100 points in a season, playing on a potent line with wingers Al Secord and Steve Larmer for most of the time, Savard was traded to the Canadiens in 1990 in exchange for Chris Chelios. In his third and final season in Montreal, the Habs won the Stanley Cup.

"When I got to Montreal, Mathieu Schneider was wearing 18, but (general manager) Serge

asked him if he would give me 18 and then asked me if I would wear it," says Savard. "I was honoured."

The next year, after the Cup win, Savard was moved to Tampa where he wore 9 for a season (because Rob Dimaio had 18). He switched to 18 the following season, but was traded back to Chicago where he finished his career in 1997. Since then he has been an assistant coach with the 'Hawks, and in 2006-07 took over as head coach.

Savard finished his career as the third leading scorer in Blackhawks history. Number 18 was retired in Chicago on March 19, 1998, and Savard was inducted into the Hockey Hall of Fame in 2000.

"Lou made good on his promise that 18 was going to be good for me," says Savard.

Mel Hill

No. 18

1. **Denis Savard**, Chicago Blackhawks
2. **Serge Savard**, Montreal Canadiens
3. **Danny Gare**, Buffalo Sabres
4. **Dave Taylor,** Los Angeles Kings
5. **Ed Westfall**, Boston Bruins
6. **Marian Hossa**, Atlanta Thrashers
7. **Craig Simpson**, Edmonton Oilers
8. **Mike Ricci**, Philadelphia Flyers
9. **Walt Tkaczuk**, New York Rangers
10. **Ken Mosdell**, Montreal Canadiens

Dave Taylor

Bet You Forgot

In the 1939 playoffs, Mel Hill, wearing No. 18, earned the nickname "Sudden Death" when he scored three over-time goals for the Boston Bru-ins in a seven-game semifinal with the New York Rangers. He never scored another overtime goal again.

Says:

"Probably one of the hardest one-on-one players to play against. Denis had great agility and puckhandling skills, and was a tremendous competitor."

Greg Millen

Serge Savard

Steve Yzerman

He will always be remembered for the number 19 on his back and the Detroit Red Wing on his chest, which he wore from start to finish in his career.

But once upon a time, a young Steve Yzerman wore a different famous number.

"When I was a little, little kid," says the Detroit legend, "I was number 4 for Bobby Orr."

But as he was growing up near Ottawa, long after Orr had retired, Yzerman added another favourite player to his list and, as a result, switched his allegiance to 19.

"I think I first wore it in Tier II in Nepean as a 15-year-old," he says. "And the reason I chose it, is that when Bryan Trottier first came into the league I followed him and Mike Bossy very closely and they became, after Bobby Orr, my two favourite players.

"I became a centreman about the same time Bryan came into the NHL and I just admired and liked the way he played. I was a big New York Islanders fan and always wanted to be like him. Back then, when I was a kid, the numbers only went up to 15. So it wasn't until I went to Tier II, where there were higher numbers, that I could make the switch to 19 and I did. I was always 14 before that."

It is fair to say Yzerman succeeded in his goal of being just like Trottier and arguably better. And the kid who was number 4 for Bobby Orr has left his own legacy in Detroit where number 19 will always be linked to Steve Yzerman.

A first pick of the Red Wings in 1983, essentially because the Islanders took Detroit native Pat LaFontaine before him, Yzerman quickly established his worth in the Motor City. He had 87 points in his rookie season and went on to a career-best 155 points in 1988-89. At the age of 21 he was named captain and set the league record of 20 years as the longest-serving captain with just one team.

While it took several years to accomplish the feat, Yzerman led the Red Wings to three Stanley Cup victories. The first came in 1997, ending a 42-year drought in Detroit. There was another in 1998, in which he won the Conn Smythe Trophy, and a third in 2002. Along the way, he won the Lester B. Pearson Award in 1989 and was named the league's top defensive forward in 2000, a testament to his great two-way skills.

When he retired in the summer of 2006, Yzerman stood sixth on the NHL's all-time scoring list with 1,755 points, including 692 goals (eighth all-time) and 1,063 assists (seventh all-time).

Number 19 was retired by the Red Wings on January 2, 2007.

Hockey Night Says:

"The greatest players to wear the number 19 share the ability to score a big goal like Joe Sakic, to win a big faceoff like Bryan Trottier, to risk injury with a big shot block or great defensive play like Larry Robinson. You would want all of them to be your captain. Steve Yzerman embodies all of those qualities."

Jim Hughson

No. 19

1. **Steve Yzerman**, Detroit Red Wings
2. **Joe Sakic**, Colorado Avalanche
3. **Larry Robinson**, Montreal Canadiens
4. **Bryan Trottier**, New York Islanders
5. **Jean Ratelle,** New York Rangers
6. **Rick MacLeish**, Philadelphia Flyers
7. **Butch Goring**, Los Angeles Kings
8. **Paul Henderson**, Toronto Maple Leafs
9. **Joe Thornton**, San Jose Sharks
10. **Brad Richards**, Tampa Bay Lightning

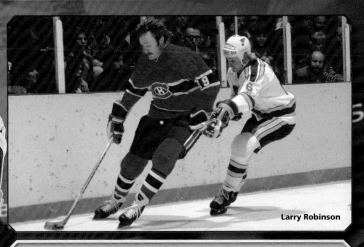

Larry Robinson

Joe Thornton

Bet You Forgot

San Jose Sharks star Joe Thornton, who grew up in London, Ontario, was a Leafs fan as a kid but wears No. 19 because his favourite player was the Red Wings great Steve Yzerman. Thornton said although he liked the Leafs, he went to a lot of games in Detroit because Red Wings tickets were easier than Leafs tickets to acquire. As a boy he originally wore No. 2 because his father's favourite player was Montreal great Doug Harvey, but he switched to Yzerman's 19 when he was 11. "You don't see too many forwards wearing No. 2, so I decided to start wearing 19 and I never switched back." Thornton did wear No. 6 briefly with Boston.

Luc Robitaille

The number 20 wasn't the first number Luc Robitaille wore when he arrived at his first Los Angeles Kings training camp, but it was the last number he wore and he will be the last King to ever wear it.

"My first two years at training I was given number 56," explains Robitaille, who in the spring of 2007 was named the Kings' president of business operations. "The third year, after winning all my awards in the Quebec junior league, when I got to camp they had the number 20 at my stall. I never asked a question about it, but I was really happy I had gotten rid of 56."

Indeed, when the Montreal native was drafted by the Kings, he was selected 171st overall in 1984 and considered by many to be gifted, but too slow to be a good NHL player. Thus, the number 56. But during his time in Hull, Robitaille worked on improving his skills and became a dynamic player, voted the top junior in the country in 1986. The next fall he reported to camp, greeted by the number 20, and didn't leave the NHL until 20 years later.

"I liked the irony back then of getting 20," he says. "I took a lot of pride in it, due to the fact that I was 20 years old at the time and the franchise was 20 years old, so that meant a lot to me. I wore 20 everywhere I went throughout my career. Ray Ferraro had to give it to me twice, once in New York with the Rangers and when I got back to LA in 1997. I felt so bad that I bought him and his family a trip to Hawaii."

Money well spent, Robitaille insists.

Despite his doubters, Robitaille was the top rookie in the NHL in 1987, with 84 points in 79 games, and he scored 53 goals in his sophomore season. In 1992-93, he set NHL records for a left winger, scoring 63 goals and 125 points. He scored 40 or more goals in all of his first eight seasons, the third longest streak in league history. He went on to play a season in Pittsburgh and made stops in New York, Los Angeles, and Detroit, where he won a Stanley Cup, before returning to the Kings to wrap up his career, finishing with 668 goals and 1,394 points.

One career highlight was the 1994 world championships, in which Robitaille scored the tournament-winning goal in a shootout giving Team Canada its first gold in 33 years.

Interestingly, after getting the number 20 when he was 20, in the franchise's 20th year, Robitaille had his number 20 retired on January 20th, 2007.

Says:

"Luc had a unique interest in scoring. He loved to score and that's the best thing you can say about him. He loved the game, but scoring was paramount to him."

Kelly Hrudey

No. 20

1. **Luc Robitaille**, Los Angeles Kings
2. **Ed Belfour**, Dallas Stars
3. **Dino Ciccarelli**, Minnesota North Stars
4. **Pete Mahovlich**, Montreal Canadiens
5. **Mickey Redmond**, Detroit Red Wings
6. **Gary Suter**, Calgary Flames
7. **Bob Pulford**, Toronto Maple Leafs
8. **Al Secord**, Chicago Blackhawks
9. **Ray Ferraro**, Los Angeles Kings
10. **Anton Stastny**, Quebec Nordiques

Ryan Suter

Bet You Forgot

Tradition often plays a part in the numbers players choose, and so it is for Nashville's Ryan Suter, who wears No. 20 because both his father and uncle won championships wearing that number. Ryan's father Bob won a gold medal with Team USA at the 1980 Olympics and his uncle, Gary, won a Stanley Cup with the Calgary Flames in 1989.

Dino Ciccarelli

Stan Mikita

When he was younger, just starting his NHL career, Stan Mikita wondered what the secret to a long career would be.

"I remember asking Ted Lindsay," says Mikita. "He just said, 'Kid, hit 'em first'".

Mikita took the advice to heart and apparently it worked, or helped, because he went on to enjoy a remarkable 22-year career with the Blackhawks, establishing himself as one of the top players all-time and making number 21 famous in Chicago.

"There's a real good story behind my number, it's the sweater they gave me," says Mikita. "When I came up from St. Catharines, I was an 18-year-old punk and 18-year-old punks didn't ask questions. At the time, the numbers only really went up to 17 or 18, but that's what they gave me, 21. I think John McKenzie wore it before me. It was one of the higher numbers at the time. Bobby Baun had it in Toronto and I think that was it.

"In junior, I wore 10 for a while. Same reason, that's what they gave me. I was a 16-year-old punk then."

It was after a great junior career with the St. Catharines Teepees that Mikita moved up to the Blackhawks, where he won a Stanley Cup in 1961, and quickly established himself as one of the best offensive players in the NHL. Playing on what was called the Scooter Line with Ken Wharram and Ab McDonald (and later Doug Mohns), Mikita won the Hart Trophy twice, the scoring title four times and after changing his style of play midway through his career—because he was taking too many penalties—he won the Lady Byng trophy as most gentlemanly player twice. Indeed, he is the only player ever to be the most valuable player, most gentlemanly player, and scoring champion in the same season and he did it twice.

His best season was 1966-67 when he finished with 97 points. Mikita was noted for not just being a great scorer, though. He was also solid defensively and excellent on faceoffs. He had two trademarks during his career, the first being the big curved blade on his stick, and the other the bubble-shaped helmet he wore.

Mikita retired in 1980 and is 13th all-time in NHL scoring with 1,467 points. Nicknamed Stosh because of his Slovakian heritage, Mikita was inducted into the Hockey Hall of Fame in 1983.

He also gained notoriety of a different kind when his name was used in the movie *Wayne's World*. In a take-off on Tim Hortons coffee shops, the doughnut shop in the movie was called Stan Mikita's.

No. 21

1. **Stan Mikita**, Chicago Blackhawks
2. **Peter Forsberg**, Colorado Avalanche
3. **Borje Salming**, Toronto Maple Leafs
4. **Bobby Baun**, Toronto Maple Leafs
5. **Guy Carbonneau**, Montreal Canadiens
6. **Adam Oates**, Detroit Red Wings
7. **Doug Jarvis**, Montreal Canadiens
8. **Butch Goring**, New York Islanders
9. **Brent Sutter**, New York Islanders
10. **Dennis Maruk**, Washington Capitals

Jerry Toppazzini

Bet You Forgot

Not too many players who have strapped on the pads to play goal have worn No. 21, but Jerry Toppazzini did on November 16, 1960, for the Boston Bruins. Goaltender Don Simmons was injured in the final minute and with no other goalie available, Toppazzini was sent to the net, becoming the last player in NHL history to be switched to goalie during a game.

Peter Forsberg

*"Stan Mikita was one of the great stickhandlers. Funny story about Stan. In his first year in the NHL—
and I played junior against him—he was a miserable son of a gun. He got a lot of penalties. His daughter,
I guess, got mad when she saw her Dad going to the penalty box so often and so he just reversed his form,
not on talent, just all of a sudden he was a candidate for the Lady Byng Trophy. It was an amazing turnaround
because he had a dirty streak when he started. He was a real skilled player and one of those guys who
hung on to the puck until the last second and made the good play."*

Mike Bossy

Think sniper and you instantly think Mike Bossy.

A gifted goal scorer even as a 14-year-old junior in Laval, Bossy was a top scorer with the New York Islanders as well, noted for his quick release and terrific shot.

Indeed, after being selected 15th overall in the 1977 draft by the Isles, Bossy set a rookie record at the time with 53 goals playing on a line with Bryan Trottier and Clark Gillies. Needless to say he won the Calder Trophy, a heady achievement for a youngster scouts thought might not have the fortitude to compete in the NHL.

For nine straight seasons he scored 50 goals or more, something only Wayne Gretzky has done—though not in consecutive seasons. Bossy scored an amazing 50 goals in 50 games in 1980-81, the first time that feat had been accomplished since Rocket Richard in 1944-45.

In four of those high-scoring years, Bossy scored more than 60 goals, including 69 in 1978-79. And despite the rap against him dating back to junior that he was a one-dimensional player, with the Islanders he established himself as a good defensive player as well. He was the complete package.

When back injuries forced him to retire at age 30 after just 10 seasons, Bossy had helped to make the Islanders a dynasty, leading them to four Stanley Cup victories in the early 1980s. He won the Conn Smythe Trophy once and the Lady Byng Trophy three times.

Overall, the Montreal native finished with 1,126 regular-season points, including 573 goals. He added another 85 goals in the playoffs, including 17 in three straight springs.

In 1991, he was inducted into the Hockey Hall of Fame and number 22 was retired by the Islanders on March 3, 1992.

"There was nothing scientific about the number," says Bossy. "I wore 17 through junior. My brother Roddy wore 17 with Halifax Junior Canadiens and someone said I should wear it as well. When I got to the Islanders, 17 was taken. Jude Drouin had it. Since he didn't say, 'here's the number,' I had three to choose from: 7, 16, and 22. Since 22 (January 22, 1957) was my birthday, that's what I took.

"About two months later Drouin got traded, but by then I had 20 goals, so there was no reason to change."

No. 22

1. **Mike Bossy**, New York Islanders
2. **John Ferguson**, Montreal Canadiens
3. **Steve Shutt**, Montreal Canadiens
4. **Rick Tocchet**, Philadelphia Flyers
5. **Rick Vaive**, Toronto Maple Leafs
6. **Dave Williams**, Toronto Maple Leafs
7. **Brad Park**, Boston Bruins
8. **Dino Ciccarelli**, Washington Capitals
9. **Charlie Huddy**, Edmonton Oilers
10. **Claude Lemieux**, Colorado Avalanche

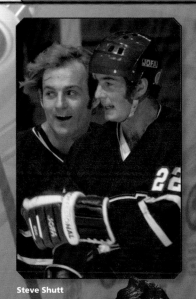

Steve Shutt

Says:

"I think Mike is the purest goal scorer that I ever played against and that obviously would only have been in practices. He was just a remarkable goal scorer with a knack of finding the openings and clearly had the quickest release I have ever seen in my life."

Kelly Hrudey

Brad Park

Les Costello

Bet You Forgot

There are few NHL players who would qualify for priesthood, but Les Costello was one of them. After a brief career with the Toronto Maple Leafs in the late 1940s, Costello, who wore 22, entered the church and became a Catholic priest. However, he never lost his love of hockey and he founded the Flying Fathers, an all-priest hockey team that played exhibition games to raise money for charity.

Bob Gainey

"I consider Bob Gainey the world's best all-around player."

That heady praise came from former Soviet coach Viktor Tikhonov in 1981.

Indeed, although he was a defensive specialist supreme, the former Montreal Canadiens winger was a terrific all-around player during his 16-year NHL career. He was a relentless checker and a great leader.

With the Canadiens, who made him their first pick, eighth overall in 1973, Gainey won the Stanley Cup five times and was awarded the Selke Trophy, as top defensive forward, four consecutive years, the first four years it was awarded in fact.

The Peterborough native also won the Conn Smythe Trophy in 1979. He was named captain in 1981 and was elected to the Hockey Hall of Fame in 1992, finishing his career with 239 goals and 262 assists.

"I think I was given number 23," recalls Gainey. "And because I was a pretty quiet kid, I put it on happily and didn't make a peep.

"I wore number 14 in junior with the Peterborough Petes. It was also available in Montreal, but it was handed to Glenn Goldup. So that's how it went.

"Certain sweater numbers with les Canadiens would be held out of circulation when the player had retired, out of respect. Then it would be re-inserted at a later time. Serge Savard [former Habs general manager] gave number 23 to Brian Bellows when he was traded by Minnesota [Gainey was the North Stars general manager who traded him] to Montreal for Russ Courtnall. Not sure of Serge's motivation there?

"I believe Bob Murdoch wore number 23 before me."

After his playing days in Montreal, Gainey was a player/coach in France and returned to the NHL in Minnesota as coach and later general manager. He moved with the franchise to Dallas, where he won the Stanley Cup in 1999. He returned to the Canadiens as general manager in May 2003.

HOCKEY NIGHT

Says:

"I have a thick wool sweater that always reminds me of Gainey. Once on a golf trip with Bob and 100 rink rats (friends celebrating player agent Don Meehan's 50th birthday) in Ireland, I was amazed to witness Bob become the source of comfort to every member on the tour. On or off the ice, Gainey's that sweater..."

Ron MacLean

No. 23

1. **Bob Gainey**, Montreal Canadiens
2. **Bob Nystrom**, New York Islanders
3. **Eddie Shack**, Toronto Maple Leafs
4. **Brian Bellows**, Minnesota North Stars
5. **Randy Carlyle**, Toronto Maple Leafs
6. **Chris Drury**, Buffalo Sabres
7. **Dave Andreychuk**, New Jersey Devils
8. **Mathieu Schneider**, Detroit Red Wings
9. **Paul Reinhart**, Calgary Flames
10. **Thomas Gradin**, Vancouver Canucks

Serge Savard

Eddie Shack

Bet You Forgot
Montreal Canadiens legendary defenceman Serge Savard wore No. 23 during the 1972 Canada–Russia Summit Series because teammate Jean Ratelle wore 18, which was Savard's number with the Habs.

24

Chris Chelios

Few have played the game tougher, and fewer still longer, than defenceman Chris Chelios.

Having begun his career with the Montreal Canadiens in 1983, the Chicago-born Chelios' next season will be his 24th, which would tie him for third in NHL history and add new meaning to the jersey number he has worn most often.

He started his long career wearing number 24 with the Canadiens, winning a Stanley Cup with Montreal in 1986 and his first of three Norris Trophies as top defenceman in 1989. However, a blockbuster trade in 1990 saw him dealt to Chicago in exchange for Blackhawks star Denis Savard and Chelios switched to number seven, a number not available in Montreal, it having been retired in honour of Howie Morenz.

Chelios' career continued to thrive in the Windy City, winning the Norris Trophy in both 1993 and 1996 and helping the Blackhawks reach the Stanley Cup final in 1992, a series they lost to Pittsburgh.

He found himself on the move again in 1999 when he was traded to the Detroit Red Wings and, with number seven retired in Motown for Ted Lindsay, Chelios returned to his number 24, in part because of his friendship with the previous player to wear the number in Detroit: Bob Probert.

Though some thought his already long career was in decline, Chelios was rejuvenated in Detroit and won his second Stanley Cup when the Red Wings defeated the Carolina Hurricanes in the final in 2002. That season, Chelios' plus-40 led the entire league and he was named to his fifth First All-Star team.

A sure bet to be inducted into the Hall of Fame when he finally decides to retire, Chelios has his own thoughts on how he would like to be honoured. As he told *Sports Illustrated* when asked about his thoughts on death: "I'd like to die fast and painlessly at a hockey rink," he said. "I'll watch a game, have a heart attack and go. Then I want my body to be frozen and stored off I-290 in Chicago. Overhead will be a neon sign flashing my NHL numbers, 24 and 7, nonstop."

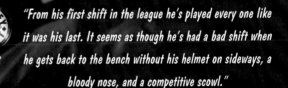

"From his first shift in the league he's played every one like it was his last. It seems as though he's had a bad shift when he gets back to the bench without his helmet on sideways, a bloody nose, and a competitive scowl."

Jim Hughson

FEDERKO WILSON O'REILLY SAWCHUK REDMOND

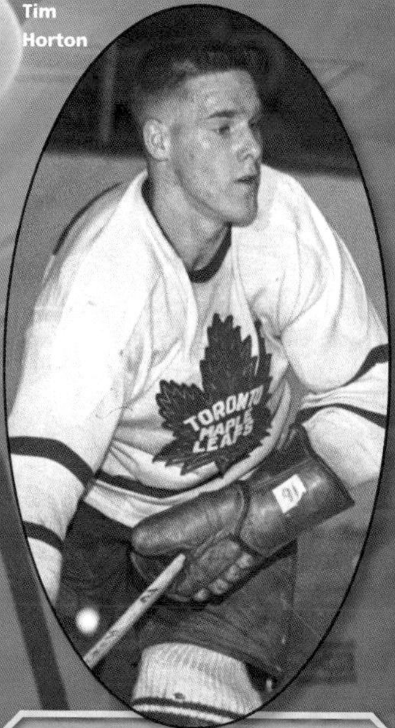

Tim Horton

No. 24

1. **Chris Chelios**, Montreal Canadiens
2. **Bernie Federko**, St. Louis Blues
3. **Doug Wilson**, Chicago Blackhawks
4. **Terry O'Reilly**, Boston Bruins
5. **Terry Sawchuk**, Toronto Maple Leafs
6. **Mickey Redmond**, Montreal Canadiens
7. **Bob Probert**, Detroit Red Wings
8. **Sergei Makarov**, San Jose Sharks
9. **Pierre Larouche**, New York Rangers
10. **Jim Peplinski**, Calgary Flames

Bet You Forgot

There is an entire generation of Canadian kids who probably only know Tim Horton as a donut store, but the man was a defensive stalwart who won four Stanley Cups with the Toronto Maple Leafs in the 1960s. But after wearing No. 2 with the Leafs for 17 full seasons, he was traded to the New York Rangers in 1970 and was subsequently chosen in a couple of post-expansion intraleague drafts, first by Pittsburgh, where he wore No. 24, and then Buffalo. He died tragically in a car accident on February 21, 1974. His No. 2 was retired by Buffalo.

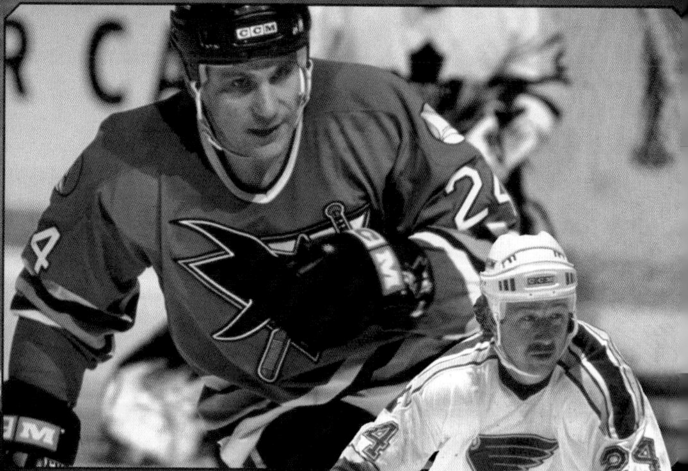

Sergei Makarov

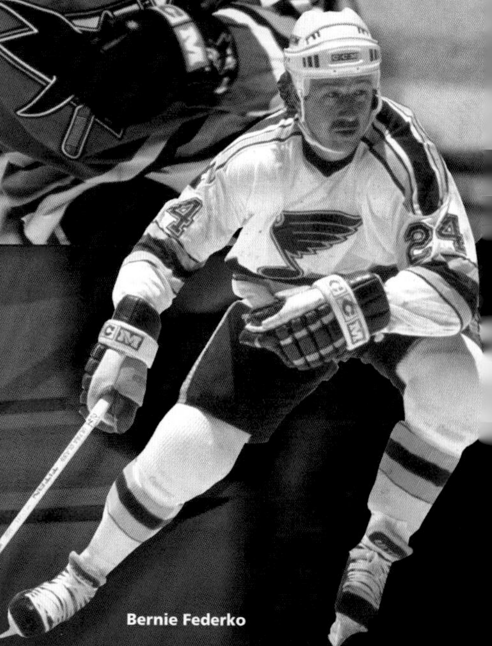

Bernie Federko

Jacques Lemaire

Winning the Stanley Cup seemed almost an annual affair for Jacques Lemaire as he hoisted the hallowed trophy eight times in his 12-year career. And he didn't have to wait too long once his career began to do it.

After serving an apprenticeship in the juniors and minor leagues—as the Montreal Canadiens were wont to do with prospects in the 1960s—Lemaire made it to the big club in the 1967-68 season, in time for the Habs to win their first of two consecutive Stanley Cups. Though a rookie, Lemaire was no passenger, scoring 22 goals in the regular season and seven more in the playoffs.

"I wore 11 in juniors because that was the number they gave me and I wore the number 25 with Canadiens because that was what I was given," says Lemaire, adding with a laugh, "but I made the number famous."

Indeed, he did. When people think of 25 and the Canadiens, they immediately think of Lemaire and the many skills he possessed.

A centre born in the Montreal suburb of Lasalle, he grew into a key cog in the Montreal machine of the 1970s, winning the Cup six more times and twice scoring the Cup-winning goal, one of just five players to accomplish the feat. None was more dramatic than the one he scored in overtime on May 14, 1977, to complete a sweep of the Boston Bruins.

His other Cup-winning goal came in 1979 against the New York Rangers.

Though he might have been overshadowed on a team filled with superstars, the quiet Lemaire put up some impressive numbers in his career, three times surpassing 90 points and scoring a career-high 44 goals in 1972-73. He finished his career with 366 goals and 835 points in 853 games, and was inducted into the Hockey Hall of Fame in 1984.

Following the 1979 Cup, Lemaire left the NHL to play and coach in Switzerland, preparing for his second NHL career as a coach. His first assignment was as assistant coach with his Canadiens in 1983-84, but after being head coach the following season, Lemaire moved to the front office becoming, among other duties, assistant general manager.

But the ice beckoned him back and in 1993-94 he was again behind the bench, this time with the New Jersey Devils. Once his defensive scheme was instituted, Lemaire won his ninth Stanley Cup, and first as a coach, the following season. He now coaches the Minnesota Wild.

Says:

"A fierce competitor and highly underrated. Nobody realized how intelligent he was about the game of hockey until he took up coaching. And then he's shown everybody that he knows—and knew—this game inside out, when he played it, and now when he's coaching."

Bob Cole

No. 25

1. **Jacques Lemaire**, Montreal Canadiens
2. **Joe Nieuwendyk**, Calgary Flames
3. **Dave Andreychuk**, Buffalo Sabres
4. **Thomas Steen**, Winnipeg Jets
5. **Kevin Stevens**, Pittsburgh Penguins
6. **Vincent Damphousse**, Montreal Canadiens
7. **Randy Carlyle**, Pittsburgh Penguins
8. **Keith Primeau**, Philadelphia Flyers
9. **Orland Kurtenbach**, Toronto Maple Leafs
10. **Chris Pronger**, Anaheim Ducks

Joe Nieuwendyk

Thomas Steen

Bet You Forgot

As a kid, Keith Primeau always favoured the number five and for several NHL seasons wore 55. After being traded to Philadelphia, he was forced to change numbers because Ulf Samuelsson wore 55. According to *The Little Book of Hockey Sweaters*, Primeau took 25 because it was his son Corey's number. Primeau said Corey took the 2 from his uncle Wayne's 22 and the 5 from his dad's 55.

Peter Stastny

When Peter Stastny defected from Communist Czechoslovakia in 1980, it's likely he hoped for little more than a successful hockey career. Twenty-seven years later his impact is still being felt.

Stastny, the Czech League's player of the year in 1980, fled his Soviet-controlled homeland with his brother Anton to play for the Quebec Nordiques. The next year older brother Marian joined them, making them just the third brother trio to play for the same team.

But it was number 26, Peter, who was the star. He had 109 points his first season and recorded five more 100-point outputs to follow. His prodigious pace made him the second-highest scorer, behind Wayne Gretzky, of the 1980s, and both are the only two players to score 1,000 points in a single decade.

In addition to the path he blazed for players to come to the NHL, Peter's presence in the NHL is now represented by his son Paul, a rookie with the Colorado Avalanche in 2006-07.

Though Peter's number is retired in Quebec (the Avalanche's predecessor), Paul was able to wear number 26 with Colorado after defenceman John-Michael Liles surrendered it in favour of Paul. In his first game wearing the number, Paul scored his first NHL goal.

Interestingly, prior to coming to the NHL Peter wore number 18 with his club team, but 26 with the national team. Brother Marian wound up wearing 18 in Quebec.

"I don't think numbers are a big issue, but it's that icing on the cake, that special touch to have the same number I wore my whole life and that my father had when he played in the NHL," Paul said.

Peter's other son, Yan, also plays in the NHL, and wears number 43 with the Boston Bruins.

When Peter was traded to New Jersey he briefly wore 29, but was given 26 out of respect by defenceman Tommy Albelin.

Peter, meanwhile, continues to affect change. He has been a member of the European Parliament for his native Slovakia since 2004.

Jere Lehtinen

No. 26

1. **Peter Stastny**, Quebec Nordiques
2. **Mats Naslund**, Montreal Canadiens
3. **Patrik Elias**, New Jersey Devils
4. **Martin St. Louis**, Tampa Bay Lightning
5. **Brian Propp**, Philadelphia Flyers
6. **Allan Stanley**, Toronto Maple Leafs
7. **Alexei Zhamnov**, Chicago Blackhawks
8. **Glen Wesley**, Boston Bruins
9. **Ray Ferraro**, Hartford Whalers
10. **Jere Lehtinen**, Dallas Stars

Pete Mahovlich

Bet You Forgot

This is the number Pete Mahovlich found himself wearing after he was dispatched from the Cup-champion Montreal Canadiens in the 1977-78 season to the woeful Pittsburgh Penguins. Though Mahovlich had put up big numbers wearing No. 20 with the Habs—most particularly 117 points in 1974-75, a club record for a centre—coach Scotty Bowman wasn't fond of his less-than-disciplined character and he was traded.

HOCKEY NIGHT *Says:*

"Another fierce competitor. Tremendous, tremendous vision in terms of seeing the ice. I can always remember him being difficult in terms of puck possession because he won a lot of draws."

Greg Millen

Frank Mahovlich

Known as the Big M, Frank Mahovlich was one of the top left wingers of his day.

He had a big stride and quick shot and was a prolific goal scorer, who helped lead the Toronto Maple Leafs to four Stanley Cup victories during the 1960s, including their last win in 1967.

Mahovlich was a graduate, like so many Leafs prospects, of the St. Michael's Majors. His first season with the Leafs was in 1957-58, when he scored 20 goals and won the Calder Trophy. Three seasons later, he scored 48 goals, which for many years was the closest any Leaf got to scoring 50 in a season.

Mahovlich was always among the Leafs' leading scorers and better players, but he had an on-again, off-again relationship with coach–general manager Punch Imlach.

One year, in the midst of a tough contract negotiation with the Leafs, he became the centre of a fascinating story when the Chicago Blackhawks offered $1 million for his services and believed they had made a deal, but the Leafs quickly signed Mahovlich and claimed otherwise.

The stress of his relationship with management and from playing in Toronto took its toll on Mahovlich, who was eventually traded in 1968 to the Detroit Red Wings along with Pete Stemkowski, Gary Unger, and the rights to Carl Brewer for Norm Ullman, Paul Henderson, Floyd Smith, and Doug Barrie.

Mahovlich rejuvenated his career in Detroit, scoring 49 goals in 1968-69. He was traded to Montreal in 1971 and helped win two Stanley Cups for the Canadiens.

Mahovlich, who played for Team Canada in the 1972 Summit Series, eventually wound up in the World Hockey Association before retiring in 1979 with 533 goals and 1,103 points in his 18 NHL seasons.

Throughout his NHL career, Mahovlich wore 27, but briefly wore number 26 when he was called up to the Leafs in 1956-57 out of junior.

Mahovlich was inducted into the Hockey Hall of Fame in 1981 and appointed to the Senate in Canada in 1988. His number 27 was honoured by the Leafs, but not retired, in 2001.

No. 27

1. **Frank Mahovlich**, Toronto Maple Leafs
2. **Darryl Sittler**, Toronto Maple Leafs
3. **Scott Niedermayer**, New Jersey Devils
4. **John Tonelli**, New York Islanders
5. **Reggie Leach**, Philadelphia Flyers
6. **Ron Hextall**, Philadelphia Flyers
7. **Jeremy Roenick**, Chicago Blackhawks
8. **Michael Peca**, Buffalo Sabres
9. **Gilles Meloche**, Minnesota North Stars
10. **Shayne Corson**, Montreal Canadiens

Scott Niedermayer

Paul Stewart

Says:

"Probably the strongest-looking skater, and most explosive skater on the left side, the Toronto Maple Leafs ever had. And he a great shot. When he was in the mood to play the game, there were none better."

Bob Cole

Bet You Forgot

Former NHL referee Paul Stewart wore No. 27 during his brief 21-game career (two goals, 74 penalty minutes) as a player in the 1979-80 season with the Quebec Nordiques. He would go on to greater prominence as an NHL referee. Indeed, Stewart had the distinction of being the first American-born NHL player to become an NHL referee. Stewart officiated his 1,000th NHL game on March 15, 2003, in Boston. His grandfather, Bill Stewart, was the first American-born referee in the NHL. His father and brother were also officials.

Steve Larmer

Sometimes, Steve Larmer believes, it's best just to take what they give you and don't ask questions.

"Especially when you're picked in the sixth round," jokes the native of Peterborough, Ontario.

But for a player who was selected 120th overall in 1980 by the Chicago Blackhawks, he no doubt surprised a few people by assembling a very impressive professional career, although it shouldn't have been a complete shock because he was a high-scoring junior.

"My training camp number in Chicago was 56," said Larmer. "You know when you get the big number you have no chance of making it, at least that year."

After a good junior career that started in his hometown and ended after three more seasons in Niagara Falls, the right winger played a handful of games with the Hawks but essentially started his pro career in Moncton, playing a season for the New Brunswick Hawks, where they won the AHL championship.

"When I got to Chicago again they gave me 28, which was better than 56," he said. "There was no significance to wearing that number, it's what they gave me that year when I showed up."

That turned out to be quite a season, too. Larmer had 43 goals and 90 points his rookie season, playing on a line with the dynamic Denis Savard and rugged Al Secord. He won the Calder Trophy.

From that point on, Larmer never missed a game for 11 straight seasons in Chicago, playing 884 consecutive games for the Blackhawks. During that time he scored 40 or more goals five times, set a team record for right wingers with 101 points in a season, and played in two all-star games.

Larmer was traded to New York (via Hartford) in 1994 and helped lead the Rangers to their first Stanley Cup in 54 years. He also played in the 1991 Canada Cup as well as the world championships. He retired in 1995 with 441 goals and 1,012 points to his credit.

"In junior I wore the number 8, but for no reason," he said. "It's what they gave me my first year with the Petes and in Niagara Falls they gave it to me there, too. In Moncton, they gave me 16, which was my favourite number for Derek Sanderson. I really liked the way he played, tenacious on the forecheck.

"But the number wasn't a big deal with me. Hey, when you're drafted in the sixth round there's not a whole lot you ask for. I didn't even get a signing bonus, so I wasn't going to push it on the number. I'm certainly not complaining about the way it turned out."

LAROUCHE   LARSON   SANDSTROM
DESJARDINS   BREWER

No. 28

1. **Steve Larmer**, Chicago Blackhawks
2. **Pierre Larouche**, Montreal Canadiens
3. **Eric Desjardins**, Montreal Canadiens
4. **Reed Larson**, Detroit Red Wings
5. **Carl Brewer**, Toronto Maple Leafs
6. **Tomas Sandstrom**, New York Rangers
7. **Brian Rafalski**, New Jersey Devils
8. **Steve Duchesne**, Los Angeles Kings
9. **Martin Straka**, Florida Panthers
10. **Kjell Samuelsson**, Philadelphia Flyers

Steve Duchesne

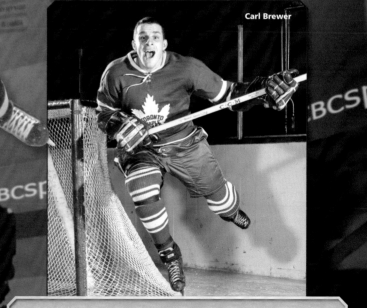

Carl Brewer

Says:

"He had a very deceptive shot. It was always a cat-and-mouse game when you played against him. He had a great delay in his backswing on his shot. He was very intelligent on the ice and he would play hurt. He was a consummate team player."

Greg Millen

Bet You Forgot

Of the many strange moves the Toronto Maple Leafs made in the late 1970s and early 1980s, one of the strangest was the return of defenceman Carl Brewer in the 1978-79 season after five years in retirement. Lured back by GM Punch Imlach, who had coached him during the team's Cup-winning years in the 1960s, Brewer wore No. 28 for 20 games before retiring again.

Ken Dryden

Ken Dryden will always be remembered for the pose.

No matter how tight the game, how dramatic the moment, the lanky Dryden always looked the picture of calm, leaning his chin on his arms crossed over the knob and top of his stick during breaks in the action. Indeed, Dryden was a calm performer and money player for the Montreal Canadiens.

Dryden was actually drafted by the Boston Bruins, but the Cornell graduate refused to report in 1964 and was subsequently traded to Montreal for Guy Allen and Paul Reid, neither of whom played in the NHL. Dryden, of course, made his memorable, storybook debut with the Canadiens in March 1971, called up at the end of the season to allow starter Rogatien Vachon a rest.

Dryden won all six games he started and Canadiens coach Al MacNeil was so impressed with Dryden and how the team played in front of him that he played a hunch and started him against Boston in the first round. Incredibly, Dryden took over the number one job and led the Canadiens to an unexpected Stanley Cup victory, winning the Conn Smythe Trophy as most valuable player in the process.

The following year Dryden won the Calder Trophy as top rookie. Dryden played from 1971 to 1979, missing the 1973-74 season because of a contract dispute, during which he spent the year articling at a law firm. In total, he won six Stanley Cups with the Canadiens in eight seasons and won the Vezina Trophy five times. He had 46 shutouts and a 2.24 career goals-against average.

Dryden was given the number 29 when he was called up from the Nova Scotia Voyageurs.

"Most goalies wore either number 1 or 30 and those were taken so I got number 29," explains Dryden. "Every goalie wants to wear number 1. When it finally became available I rushed home to tell my wife, Lynda, and she said, 'You can't wear number 1, you're number 29!'"

Ironically, the man Dryden replaced in the Canadiens goal that memorable spring in 1971—Vachon, who wore number 30—had previously worn number 29.

Dryden was inducted into the Hockey Hall of Fame in 1983 and had his number retired by the Canadiens on January 29, 2007.

Mike Vernon

No. 29

1. **Ken Dryden**, Montreal Canadiens
2. **Peter Stastny**, New Jersey Devils
3. **Mike Vernon**, Detroit Red Wings
4. **Felix Potvin**, Toronto Maple Leafs
5. **Joel Otto**, Calgary Flames
6. **Mike Palmateer**, Toronto Maple Leafs
7. **Dave Andreychuk**, Buffalo Sabres
8. **Jim Rutherford**, Detroit Red Wings
9. **Glen Hanlon**, St. Louis Blues
10. **Greg Millen**, Pittsburgh Penguins

Says:

"The guy that showed he could step from anywhere right into the hot water, like he did when he was a rookie. He played only six games (in the regular season) and took on the role of goaltending for the Canadiens against Boston in the playoffs in '71. He went on from there to show that he was one of the top goaltenders of all time. Intelligent, very smart, and one of the very best conditioned athletes."

Bob Cole

Terry Sawchuk

Bet You Forgot
There seemed to be far less sentimentality about numbers 40 years ago than there is today. Goaltender Terry Sawchuk was a star wearing No. 1 for the Detroit Red Wings in the 1950s and 60s before trades and expansion sent him to Toronto and Los Angeles. But when he returned to Detroit in 1968, his No. 1 was being worn by Roger Crozier, so Sawchuk put on No. 29 for his final 13 appearances in a Red Wings jersey.

Martin Brodeur

You could say the Devil made him do it. Or more accurately, the Devils. That, in a nutshell, is why one of the greatest goaltenders in NHL history wears the number 30. Because the New Jersey Devils—more specifically, club president, general manager, and occasional coach, Lou Lamoriello—told him to.

"I had no choice," says Brodeur. "I play for the Devils and Lou decides who wears what. And so the number 30, that was his pick." And it didn't bother Brodeur one bit. He was just glad to be playing in the NHL and as a kid he hadn't really had an idol whose number he just had to wear.

"Not really," he continues. "I started with 29 in my first couple games in the NHL, when I came up from junior, and I came back the following year and 30 was in my stall, so I didn't have a choice, really. As a kid, I had number one, I think goalies are number one, my Dad wore number one when he played, and one is always a goalie. But I didn't have the chance to wear that number."

His father is noted hockey photographer Denis Brodeur, who was also a goaltender with Canada's bronze medal-winning Olympic team in 1956.

As for the number 30, it was simply because of Lou Lamoriello?

"Because of that and the Devils," said Brodeur.

If not in sweater number, then Brodeur for many years has been number one amongst goaltenders in the NHL, especially after Patrick Roy retired. Brodeur, who was the Devils' first pick, 20th overall in 1990, has had incredible success, leading New Jersey to three Stanley Cup victories and to the playoffs in all but one of his 13 years there. Brodeur has a very good chance, if he can maintain his health, of breaking Roy's records for wins, games played, minutes played, and playoff shutouts, as well as Terry Sawchuk's record for career shutouts.

He has been an absolute workhorse throughout his career, playing a record 78 games in 2006-07. For 11 straight years he has won more than 30 games. Six times, including three of the past four seasons, he has won more than 40 games. No one else has managed that feat. He has won the Vezina Trophy three times, the Jennings Trophy four times, won the Calder as top rookie, and won gold with Canada in the 2002 Olympics.

And as if stopping pucks isn't enough, in 1997 he became just the second goaltender ever to score a goal in the playoffs.

You can bet that the number 30 Lou Lamoriello gave him to wear will never be worn by any other Devil.

No. 30

1. **Martin Brodeur**, New Jersey Devils
2. **Terry Sawchuk**, Toronto Maple Leafs
3. **Bernie Parent**, Philadelphia Flyers
4. **Mike Vernon**, Calgary Flames
5. **Gerry Cheevers**, Boston Bruins
6. **Lorne Worsley**, Montreal Canadiens
7. **Rogatien Vachon**, Los Angeles Kings
8. **Tom Barrasso**, Buffalo Sabres
9. **Bill Ranford**, Edmonton Oilers
10. **Cesare Maniago**, Minnesota North Stars

Bernie Parent

Bet You Forgot

The number 30 lives in infamy in Boston. It was worn by goaltender Dave Reece the night he was victimized for a record 10 points by the Maple Leafs' Darryl Sittler. The appearance proved to be the last of Reece's 14-game NHL career. He was assigned to the minors two days later.

Says:

"One thing he's really mastered is the mental part of the game. Physically he's very athletic, but I've seen better technical goalies. But I think he's always understood how to prepare mentally and I think that that's one of the greatest assets he's always had."

Kelly Hrudey

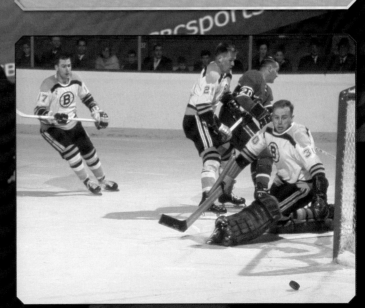

Gerry Cheevers

Grant Fuhr

Wayne Gretzky always used to say when the game was on the line, there was no better goaltender than Grant Fuhr.

"He might give up three or four goals, but if you needed him to shut the door he would," says Gretzky. "And when we needed him most in the playoffs, he was always there."

Indeed, Fuhr was noted for his cool demeanour and his ability to produce big saves in pressure games.

Drafted eighth overall by the Oilers in 1981, Fuhr won the Stanley Cup five times in Edmonton, winning the Vezina Trophy in 1988. In Edmonton, Fuhr made the number 31 his signature.

"I wore 31 in junior in Victoria and a bit as a kid," says the soft-spoken Fuhr. "I just liked the number. When I first got to Edmonton (in 1981), Eddie Mio had it, so I had to wait a bit to get it. I wore number 1 my first year, then 31 after that."

Like so many of the Oiler greats, however, he too eventually had to leave. His first stop was Toronto in 1991 as part of a multi-player trade, with moves after that to Buffalo, Los Angeles, St. Louis, Calgary, and retirement in the fall of 2000.

Fuhr also enjoyed success internationally, most notably in the historic 1987 Canada Cup, in which he allowed goals, but helped preserve two big wins in the final against the Soviets.

He finished his career with 403 wins and a 3.38 goals-against average.

"There wasn't anyone in particular who wore 31 that I liked," says Fuhr. "I always liked Tony Esposito and Glenn Hall was my favourite. I just liked the number 31 and was able to put my stamp on it, which is a good thing. It seemed to have a bit of luck for me."

The number 31 was retired in Edmonton on October 9, 2003, in honour of Fuhr, who was inducted into the Hockey Hall of Fame the following month.

Bill Smith

No. 31

1. **Grant Fuhr**, Edmonton Oilers
2. **Bill Smith**, New York Islanders
3. **Curtis Joseph**, St. Louis Blues
4. **Ed Giacomin**, Detroit Red Wings
5. **Pelle Lindberg**, Philadelphia Flyers
6. **Mark Napier**, Montreal Canadiens
7. **Rejean Lemelin**, Calgary Flames
8. **Ken Wregget**, Toronto Maple Leafs
9. **Sean Burke**, Florida Panthers
10. **Ron Tugnutt**, Ottawa Senators

Curtis Joseph

Says:

"Pure athleticism. There's a guy that everybody said is supercool and relaxed. I would probably not disagree with that, but I think that more than that he was a far better competitor than most people gave him credit for. He was just an incredible athlete and used that athleticism to his advantage."

Kelly Hrudey

Bet You Forgot
Ed Giacomin wore No. 31 with the Detroit Red Wings for the final three years of his career after wearing No. 1 for 11 seasons with the New York Rangers. Jim Rutherford had No. 1 in Detroit when Giacomin arrived in 1975-76.

Dale Hunter

Dale Hunter once said, when his career was over, he would like to be remembered for having won the Stanley Cup.

That didn't happen, of course, but Hunter is remembered for something else quite honourable, for being a guy who worked hard every night and left nothing in the dressing room. It was always about winning for the native of Petrolia, Ontario.

Hunter was a gritty, hard-working centre who was fearless. He could score goals, had a knack for scoring really important goals, and spent his fair share of time in the penalty box for his transgressions.

Drafted 41st overall by the Quebec Nordiques in 1979, the 5-foot-10, 200-pound centre wasn't given much chance of making the team when he first arrived on the scene. But what he lacked in pure talent, he made up with guts and guile.

"When I went to training camp as a 19-year-old they really didn't think I was going to make the team then," says Hunter, who now co-owns and coaches the London Knights of the Ontario Hockey League. "That's why they gave me 32. They didn't think I was going to make the team, so they gave me a high number. Back then 32 was a high number.

"When I made the team wearing that number, I thought I had better keep it the rest of my career. It brought me good luck."

Hunter wound up spending seven seasons in Quebec, where he was loved by his teammates and the fans. But management decided to trade him to Washington in 1987. The return was a draft pick that turned out to be Joe Sakic, but the loss of leadership was felt.

In Washington, Hunter was eventually named captain. His time with the Capitals was memorable, for reasons both good and bad. While he was able to surpass the 300-goal and 1,000-point plateaus and help lead the Caps to the Stanley Cup final for the first time in 1998, he also achieved infamy for a nasty, late hit on New York Islanders centre Pierre Turgeon, who had just scored a goal in the playoff series. Hunter was suspended for 21 games, but the play in many ways showed what Hunter was all about: competitive, always playing on the edge, hating to lose.

The number 32 he was given by the Nordiques was retired by the Capitals on March 11, 2000. One of the gifts he was given by the team was a penalty box, kind of fitting for a guy who had the most penalty minutes of any player to reach 1,000 career points.

The Caps traded Hunter in 1999 to Colorado—revisiting his Nordiques roots—for one last kick at winning the Stanley Cup, but the Avalanche came up short.

No. 32

1. **Dale Hunter**, Quebec Nordiques
2. **Claude Lemieux**, Montreal Canadiens
3. **Steve Thomas**, Toronto Maple Leafs
4. **Kelly Hrudey**, Los Angeles Kings
5. **Mike Vernon**, Florida Panthers
6. **Trevor Linden**, New York Islanders
7. **Craig MacTavish**, Boston Bruins
8. **Murray Craven**, Vancouver Canucks
9. **Stephane Matteau**, Chicago Blackhawks
10. **Don Sweeney**, Boston Bruins

Claude Lemieux

Gary Roberts

Says:

"To me, he was the extreme on wanting to win. His passion to win sometimes, like me, overrode his common sense. He wanted to win so bad he would do things he shouldn't have. He's one of those guys everyone hated, but deep down everyone loved. I remember I asked him why he thought he hadn't been considered for the Hockey Hall of Fame and he said 'I'm not their kind.' Great guy."

Don Cherry

Bet You Forgot

There was a fitting symmetry to the beginning of Gary Roberts' career, as he wore No. 32 for 32 games his first season with the Calgary Flames in 1986-87. Though he switched to No. 10 the following season, he by no means played the same number of games. He emerged into a star power forward and was a key ingredient in the Flames' 1989 Stanley Cup championship.

Patrick Roy

If Patrick Roy had had his way early in his career, the banner that bears his name in the rafters of Denver's Pepsi Center would have the number 30 on it, rather than 33.

Thirty was the number Roy had always worn growing up in Quebec City and while playing with the junior Granby Bisons, but when the young goaltender was called up to the Montreal Canadiens on February 23, 1985, it was already being worn.

Habs enforcer Chris Nilan had number 30. The rookie quietly took on number 33 and proceeded to make it famous.

"My first training camp, they gave me number 32 and I didn't like it," says Roy. "And Nilan had 30. At my second training camp I asked for 33 instead and that was it."

In his first and only game in 1984–85, Roy replaced starter Doug Soetart to begin the third period and earned his first win when the Canadiens rallied for a 6-4 victory. As a rookie, he helped lead the Canadiens to a Stanley Cup win in 1986 and captured the Conn Smythe Trophy.

Roy would win 551 games over the course of his career, retiring in 2003 as the NHL's career leader in victories and with four Stanley Cups, three Conn Smythe Trophies, and three Vezina Trophies.

His career, though, was not without its controversies, none more so than the night of December 2, 1995, when, after being left in for nine goals by coach Mario Tremblay in an 11-1 loss to Detroit, he leaned over the bench and told team president Ronald Corey that he had played his last game as a Canadien. Four days later he was traded to Colorado.

After having journeyman defenceman Anders Myrvold switch to number 55 so Roy could have his familiar 33, the goaltender would win two more Stanley Cups with the Avalanche, in 1996 and 2001.

When Roy retired in 2003, among the NHL records he held were most wins (551), most games played by a goalie (1,029), as well as playoff games played by a goaltender (247) and playoff wins (151).

He was inducted into the Hall of Fame in 2006 and his number 30 was retired by Granby.

No. 33

1. **Patrick Roy**, Montreal Canadiens
2. **Kris Draper**, Detroit Red Wings
3. **Don Beaupre**, Minnesota North Stars
4. **Marty McSorley**, Edmonton Oilers
5. **Ziggy Palffy**, Los Angeles Kings
6. **Sean Burke**, Philadelphia Flyers
7. **Zdeno Chara**, Boston Bruins
8. **Al Iafrate**, Toronto Maple Leafs
9. **Pete Peeters**, Philadelphia Flyers
10. **Henrik Sedin**, Vancouver Canucks

Bet You Forgot

Baseball's Justin Morneau, of the Pittsburgh Pirates, and Larry Walker, now retired—but who had great years with Colorado and St. Louis—were both goalies in their youth hockey days in British Columbia. Both wore sweater No. 33 in the majors. Morneau idolized both Patrick Roy and Walker and changed from 27 to 33 shortly after joining the Pirates. Walker is reportedly obsessed with the No. 3. He took practice swings in multiples of three, was married on Nov. 3 at 3:33 p.m., and bought tickets for 33 disadvantaged kids when he played in Montreal, to be seated in Section 333 at Olympic Stadium.

Don Beaupre

"The first time I ever played against Patrick Roy, it was in St. Louis and we had to skate past each other after he won. He sort of looked at me and winked after they beat us and I thought to myself, who is this cocky goalie anyways at such a young age? And I found out very quickly who he was. Patrick was, in our era, number one in terms of being technically sound. If you stood at the other end (in the net) it was a great challenge to play against him and you knew that if you gave him an edge in goal that nine times out of ten

34

John Vanbiesbrouck

For a guy who wasn't drafted into junior, John Vanbiesbrouck, aka "The Beezer," carved out a tremendous career for himself with stops in New York with the Rangers, Florida, Philadelphia, the Islanders, and New Jersey.

The legend of 34, the number and the player, started with the Rangers, who selected him 72nd overall in 1981. According to Vanbiesbrouck the story behind the number really isn't interesting, except...

"I wanted number 1, but couldn't have that because it belonged for so many years to Ed Giacomin," says Vanbiesbrouck, who then wanted 30 but that was formerly worn by John Davidson. Next was 31, but that was Steve Weeks' number.

"I thought that numbers 32 and 33 just seemed too odd, so I didn't want them." By then, Rangers trainer Joe "Babe" Murphy was frustrated with the young goaltender and said, "Here, kid. Take 34."

And so he did. Vanbiesbrouck debuted with the Rangers in 1981 as an 18-year-old emergency call-up, then returned to junior. He started full-time with the Rangers in 1984 and eventually formed a formidable duo with Mike Richter, who eventually took over as number one. Vanbiesbrouck was traded in 1993 to Vancouver, who left him exposed in the Expansion Draft, in which he was selected by Florida.

The Detroit native helped lead the Panthers to the Stanley Cup final in 1996, which was nice because he missed his chance with the Rangers in 1994, but Florida wound up losing in four games to Colorado.

Vanbiesbrouck retired briefly in 2001, and retired for good a year later, leaving with 374 wins and one Vezina Trophy to his credit.

"John was a good, solid goaltender."

Greg Millen

KIPRUSOFF IAFRATE COURTNALL MACOUN AUDETTE

Bet You Forgot

Vaclav Nedomansky might not have had a Hall of Fame career in the NHL, but he made his mark in 1974 when he became the first player to defect from Soviet-controlled territory to play in North America. The Czechoslovakian native fled from Switzerland to Toronto and joined the Toronto Toros of the World Hockey Association. He eventually made it to the NHL and after five seasons with Detroit and one with St. Louis, Nedomansky played his final NHL season with the New York Rangers as No. 34.

No. 34

1. **John Vanbiesbrouck**, New York Rangers
2. **Miikka Kiprusoff**, Calgary Flames
3. **Jamie Macoun**, Calgary Flames
4. **Al Iafrate,** Washington Capitals
5. **Donald Audette**, Los Angeles Kings
6. **Geoff Courtnall**, Boston Bruins
7. **Vaclav Nedomansky**, New York Rangers
8. **Scott Young**, Pittsburgh Penguins
9. **Bryan Berard**, New York Islanders
10. **Manny Legace**, Detroit Red Wings

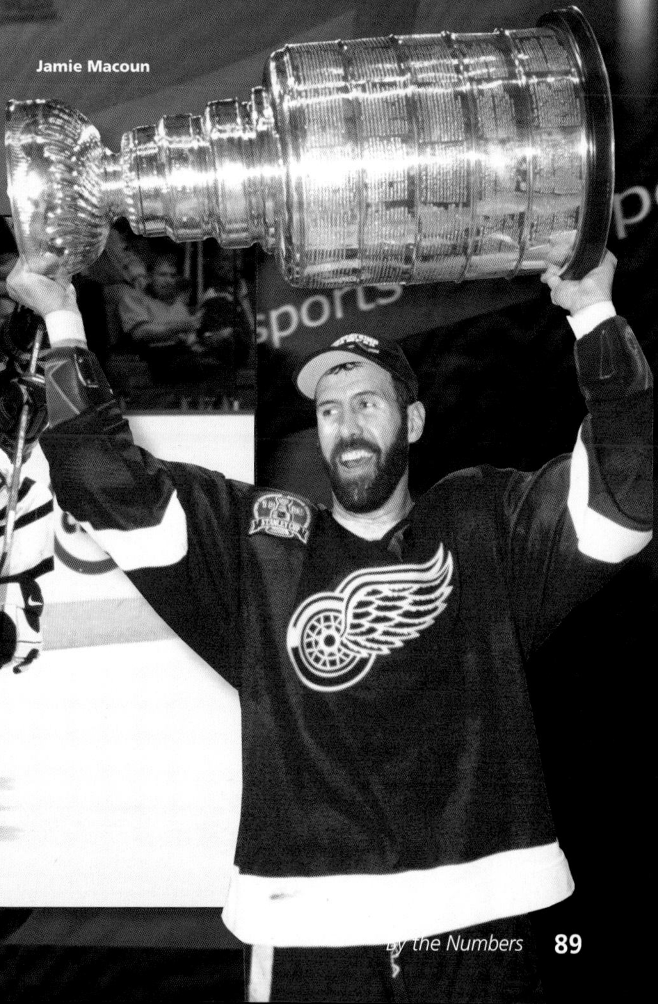

Jamie Macoun

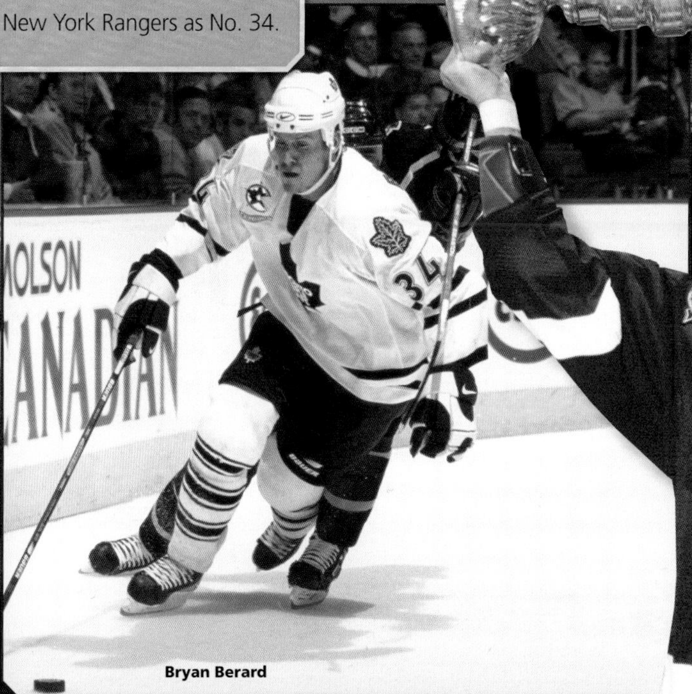

Bryan Berard

Tony Esposito

Tony Esposito was also known as Tony O because he was a very stingy goaltender.

In his rookie season, 1969-70 with the Chicago Blackhawks, the "other" Esposito brother had a 38-17-8 record with a sparkling 2.17 goals-against average and he recorded 15 shutouts, a modern-era record. He won both the Vezina and Calder Trophies, the first goalie to do that in his first season in 40 years. He was also runner-up for the Hart Trophy.

Incredibly, during his 16 seasons in the NHL, the Blackhawks never missed the playoffs with Esposito, who recorded 76 career shutouts.

In many ways, Esposito was an innovator, one of the first to perfect and popularize the "butterfly" style of falling to the knees, legs spread out. Esposito made it an art form.

Originally property of the Montreal Canadiens, he dressed for 13 games and had a 5-4-4 record with a 2.73 goals-against average. He was claimed on waivers for $25,000 by the Blackhawks

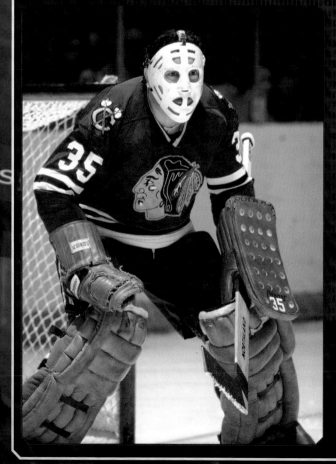

and had a terrific career in the Windy City, winning the Vezina three times and getting to the Stanley Cup final once, where he lost to Montreal. He will also be remembered for sharing the goaltending duties for Team Canada in the historic 1972 Summit Series.

According to the Hockey Hall of Fame, into which Esposito was inducted in 1988, he wanted something different in terms of a number when he got to Chicago, where Denis Dejordy wore 30 and Gerry Desjardins had number 1.

"I wanted something different," Esposito says, "something to make me stand out and for people to notice."

Mission accomplished.

The Blackhawks retired number 35 on November 20, 1988, along with the immortal Glenn Hall's number 1. Esposito was inducted into the Hockey Hall of Fame in 1988.

Bet You Forgot

Only two teams—Chicago and Minnesota—have ever had only one player wear the No. 35, to wildly differing degrees of success. Goaltender Tony Esposito wore 35 for his 15 Hall-of-Fame-calibre seasons with the Blackhawks and it was subsequently retired in his honour. Manny Fernandez, also a goaltender, wore it for the Wild, though whether it is eventually raised to the rafters remains to be seen.

No. 35

1. **Tony Esposito**, Chicago Blackhawks
2. **Andy Moog**, Edmonton Oilers
3. **Mike Richter**, New York Rangers
4. **Tom Barrasso**, Pittsburgh Penguins
5. **Jean-Sebastien Giguere**, Anaheim Ducks
6. **Marty Turco**, Dallas Stars
7. **Nikolai Khabibulin**, Tampa Bay Lightning
8. **Richard Brodeur**, Vancouver Canucks
9. **Daniel Bouchard**, Quebec Nordiques
10. **Mike McPhee**, Montreal Canadiens

Tom Barrasso

Jean-Sebastien Giguere

Says:

"Tony O came to Montreal, wasn't good enough to play for the Canadiens, and ended up playing for Chicago. It's funny, some goaltenders, in the days with the mask, are guys that come and go and you don't really remember them or notice them too much. Poor guys can't have their face to the public. But you knew that Tony Esposito was in the net every time that you saw him play with Chicago. He was a presence. The good goaltenders are and he was really a presence in the net."

Glenn Anderson

Glenn Anderson was a winner. Now, some used the term in a less-than flattering manner given his sometimes flaky behaviour, but deep down Anderson was a smart guy, a good team player, and ultimately a guy who scored big goals and won big games.

In fact, Anderson won the Stanley Cup six times, including five with the great Edmonton Oilers teams. He was a key player in those championships after joining the club in 1980 after playing with the Canadian Olympic team. In fact, that was his first goal: to make the national team, then the National Hockey League.

After 11 seasons with the Oilers, the speedy winger was traded to Toronto in 1991 as part of a package with goaltender Grant Fuhr and helped inspire a turnaround of the Leafs' fortunes. In 1994, he was traded to the New York Rangers, where he was reunited with several Oilers teammates and proceeded to win his sixth Stanley Cup.

Anderson drifted around the NHL after that, with stops in St. Louis (twice) and Edmonton, before he left the NHL after the 1995-96 season. He wound up his career with 498 goals and 601 assists, with his playoff reputation cemented by the 93 goals and 121 assists he produced in the post-season, along with five overtime goals and 17 game-winning goals.

Anderson wore 9 with the Oilers, his favoured number, but switched to 10 with the Leafs because 9 was taken by Dave Hannan. When he got to New York, centre Adam Graves had 9 and former Oiler teammate Esa Tikkanen had 10, so he got creative and wore 36, adding up the two numbers to get nine. He reverted back to 9 with St. Louis and Edmonton and finished with 36 in the final go-around with the Blues because Shayne Corson had 9.

Although his number hasn't yet been retired, Anderson will always be synonymous with success and number 9 in Edmonton.

"On par with Rocket Richard for clutch scoring and non-predictability. Automatic Hall of Fame credentials prove he can even deke the hockey moguls."

Ron MacLean

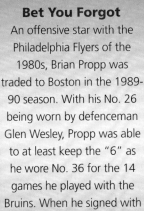

Brian Propp

No. 36

1. **Glenn Anderson**, New York Rangers
2. **Alexei Zhamnov**, Chicago Blackhawks
3. **Brian Propp**, Boston Bruins
4. **Grant Ledyard**, Boston Bruins
5. **Jussi Jokinen**, Dallas Stars
6. **Mike Eagles**, Winnipeg Jets
7. **Dmitry Yushkevich**, Toronto Maple Leafs
8. **Ron Flockhart**, Boston Bruins
9. **Murray Baron**, Montreal Canadiens
10. **Sergio Momesso**, Montreal Canadiens

Bet You Forgot

An offensive star with the Philadelphia Flyers of the 1980s, Brian Propp was traded to Boston in the 1989-90 season. With his No. 26 being worn by defenceman Glen Wesley, Propp was able to at least keep the "6" as he wore No. 36 for the 14 games he played with the Bruins. When he signed with Minnesota the following summer, 26 was also occupied, so, in keeping with his method, Propp wore No. 16 for his three seasons with the North Stars.

Alexei Zhamnov

Olie Kolzig

The road to the NHL was a long one for goaltender Olaf Kolzig, both in distance and time.

The son of German parents, Kolzig was born in Johannesburg, South Africa in 1970, though he grew up mainly in Toronto and Halifax. After a stellar junior career with the Tri-City Americans of the Western Hockey League, Kolzig was drafted 19th overall in the 1989 Entry Draft by the Washington Capitals.

However, he spent the next seven years bouncing between the NHL and the minors, unable to stick with the big club. It wasn't until the 1996-97 season that he secured himself a spot on the Capitals' roster, playing 29 games as backup to Jim Carey and Bill Ranford. In 1997-98, as his nickname "Godzilla" might suggest, Kolzig made his presence known in a big way, winning 33 games in the regular season and 12 more in the playoffs, as the surprising Capitals made it to the Stanley Cup final. Detroit would win the series in a sweep, but Kolzig had cemented himself as the Capitals' goaltender. In 1999-2000, Kolzig won a career-high 41 games, took home the Vezina Trophy as the NHL's top goaltender and was named to the First All-Star team. He says there is "no special significance" to wearing the number 37.

"I really admire this guy, that he can keep his spirits up over the years with only one trip to the finals. He continually sees more rubber than a dead cat on the Trans-Canada Highway. It's easy to be great when you're winning all the time and going to finals, but when you're continually bombarded and keep up that spirit, it takes a special guy."

Don Cherry

Bet You Forgot

Some numbers are unfortunately remembered for their connection to tragedy rather than accomplishment. Such is the case with Dan Snyder's No. 37. Snyder, a forward with the Atlanta Thrashers, was killed just before the start of the 2003-04 season when a car driven by teammate Dany Heatley crashed into a wall. His number is now prominent in helping raise funds for the Dan Snyder Memorial Foundation, set up by his parents to provide scholarship opportunities for young athletes.

No. 37

1. **Olie Kolzig**, Washington Capitals
2. **Chris Drury**, Colorado Avalanche
3. **Eric Desjardins**, Philadelphia Flyers
4. **Curtis Brown**, Buffalo Sabres
5. **Dan Snyder**, Atlanta Thrashers
6. **Patrice Bergeron**, Boston Bruins
7. **Trevor Kidd**, Calgary Flames
8. **Wes Walz**, Minnesota Wild
9. **Mark Parrish,** New York Islanders
10. **Dean McAmmond**, Ottawa Senators

Patrice Bergeron

Chris Drury

38

Dave Andreychuk

Dave Andreychuk played 23 seasons in the NHL with six different teams. He has heard a lot of stories, and he has told a lot of stories. "And every number I wore has its own story," says Andreychuk, who began his career in Buffalo as the Sabres' third choice in the first round (with Phil Housley and Paul Cyr), 16th overall in 1982.

The big winger, who usually played on the left side although he shot right, played 11 seasons in Buffalo before making stops in Toronto, New Jersey, Boston, Colorado, and Tampa Bay, where he finally won the Stanley Cup and eventually retired, joining the Lightning in their community relations department.

"My first number in Buffalo was 29," continues the Hamilton native. "Scotty Bowman gave it to me. I felt like Ken Dryden, but I was happy just to have a sweater. Then came 25. I wanted 23 for Bob Gainey, but it was taken. I always liked his style: a hard worker, smart, a great leader.

"In Toronto, I took 14. I had to choose from a few numbers but picked it because of Dave Keon. My Dad loved him.

"In New Jersey, I wore 23. I finally got it.

"In Boston, I wore 38. My daughter picked it out of some other bad choices—38, 32, 29, 42.

"In Colorado, they gave me the same number.

"Back to Buffalo and Vaclav Varada wouldn't give me 25, so I went with 52. Then it was Tampa and 25 again, which was only fitting."

Andreychuk finished his distinguished career with 640 goals and 1,338 points. His best season was in Toronto in 1993-94, when he scored 53 goals and 99 points—the latter in consecutive years.

After being traded to New Jersey, he signed with Boston as a free agent and was traded to Colorado along with Raymond Bourque, who, like Andreychuk, was looking to win his first Stanley Cup. It didn't happen that spring of 2000, but Bourque stayed in Colorado and won the Cup that next season, while Andreychuk signed as a free agent in Tampa Bay.

Interestingly, Andreychuk wound up tying Bourque for the record of most years without winning the Stanley Cup. And he was the oldest player, at 40 years and seven months, to play his first Finals game. But it was all worth the wait. In that 22nd spring, the Lightning beat the Calgary Flames in seven games and then the only number that mattered was one.

Says:

"Andreychuk was one of the best goal scorers in the NHL. He had terrific hand-eye coordination and could really tip point shots. He lived in the crease, though it wasn't very comfortable, and he could get his stick on all kinds of pucks, either on the way to the goalie or coming off the goalie. I don't know if there are very many others who scored as many goals as he did from as close in to the net."

Harry Neale

No. 38

1. **Dave Andreychuk**, Boston Bruins
2. **Pavol Demitra**, Minnesota Wild
3. **Jan Hrdina**, Pittsburgh Penguins
4. **Vladimir Malakhov**, Montreal Canadiens
5. **Mike Lalor**, Montreal Canadiens
6. **Jan Bulis**, Montreal Canadiens
7. **Vladimir Ruzicka**, Boston Bruins
8. **Lyle Odelein**, Montreal Canadiens
9. **Robbie Ftorek**, Quebec Nordiques
10. **Sean Hill**, Montreal Canadiens

Bet You Forgot

Not related, Jiri and Jan Hrdina played eight seasons apart in Pittsburgh but sported the same number. Jiri, a star with the Czech national team in the 1980s, played two seasons with the Penguins, beginning in 1990-91. Jan joined the Pens in 1998-99 and played with them for five years.

Pavol Demitra

Dominik Hasek

He will never be remembered as being a classic goaltender in terms of style, but Dominik Hasek will most certainly be remembered as one of the best in terms of performance. And results.

Unorthodox is a word that comes to mind to describe his style. He drops, he flops, he rolls around, he purposely loses his stick, and he generally just stops the puck. That is the essence of Hasek's style. Awkward, but highly effective.

Like his style, Hasek's story is an interesting one. He was the 11th pick, 199th overall of the Chicago Blackhawks in 1983, essentially because at the time the Iron Curtain hadn't yet come down so teams drafted players from communist countries late on the off-chance they might one day get them to North America. It had more to do with circumstance than skill.

When he did eventually sign with the Blackhawks in 1990, the Czechoslovakian was a backup to Ed Belfour and spent time in the minors before being shuffled off to Buffalo in a trade for Stephane Beauregard and a fourth-round draft pick, who turned out to be Eric Daze. It was while playing with the Sabres that Hasek, who had shone on the international stage previously, finally became an NHL star.

And it was in Buffalo that he first wore 39, unusual but also somehow appropriate. While with the Blackhawks, Hasek was given 34 his first season, when he appeared in just five games. The next year he was given 31.

But Hasek explained that as a kid he primarily "wore 9 in the Czech Republic because when one of our defencemen was injured, I was given his number 9."

Because he played so well wearing that number, he decided to keep it. When he went to to Buffalo in 1992 he was asked what number he wanted and he didn't really care, but knew he wanted to have a nine in it, so he said 39. At the time, 29 was occupied by Bob Corkum.

Hasek also wore number 2 while playing internationally for the former Czechoslovakia mainly "because goalies were always given either 1 or 2." And he was 2.

Whatever the number, The Dominator, as Hasek became known, has had a great career. He has won the Vezina Trophy six times, the Hart Trophy twice—the first goalie to win it in consecutive years—and the Lester B. Pearson twice.

He also won the Stanley Cup with Detroit in 2002 and led the Czech Republic to a thrilling gold-medal victory at the 1998 Winter Olympics, which included a stunning shootout win over Canada.

HOCKEY NIGHT Says:

"Dominik was the ultimate competitor and I think what made Dominik so special was his willingness to adapt to any situation. Some people would tell you that he didn't really have any style and just flopped around but I would say otherwise. I think that there was a whole method to his style and you really have to have played goal to appreciate the little things that he did to become the most dominant player for five to seven years in the National Hockey League."

Kelly Hrudey

No. 39

1. **Dominik Hasek**, Buffalo Sabres
2. **Doug Gilmour**, Calgary Flames
3. **Doug Weight**, New York Rangers
4. **Brian Skrudland**, Montreal Canadiens
5. **Joe Juneau**, Ottawa Senators
6. **Jason Spezza**, Ottawa Senators
7. **Rick DiPietro**, New York Islanders
8. **Nikolai Khabibulin**, Chicago Blackhawks
9. **Petr Sykora**, Anaheim Ducks
10. **Doug Crossman**, Detroit Red Wings

Doug Weight

Jason Spezza

Bet You Forgot

Clark Gillies went into the Hockey Hall of Fame as No. 9 of the New York Islanders, his number retired in 1996, but the rugged winger finished his career first as No. 39 with the Buffalo Sabres, then as No. 90. After 12 seasons and four Stanley Cups on Long Island, Gillies was claimed by the Sabres in the 1986 Waiver Draft. With No. 9 worn by Scott Arniel, Gillies switched to No. 39. He played two seasons with the Sabres before a knee injury in 1987 ended his career

Henrik Zetterberg

Wayne Gretzky, no less, once called him the most underrated player in the NHL.

Mike Babcock, his coach, once said he was the guy who made the Detroit Red Wings go offensively. Heady praise, indeed, for Henrik Zetterberg. But it was deserved.

Zetterberg, who was taken 210th overall in 1999 by the Red Wings, has emerged as a rising star in the NHL, having shown extended signs of greatness along the way. The young forward was allowed to play two seasons with Timra IK in Sweden after being drafted, which made the transition to pro hockey in Detroit easier, allowing him to mature as a person and a player.

Zetterberg had a terrific rookie season, too, leading all rookies with 22 goals and 44 points and finished second in balloting for the Calder Trophy. At the time, he played on a line with Brett Hull and Pavel Datsyuk, the latter with whom he has developed a terrific chemistry. It was the irreverent Hull who once referred to the line as being comprised of two kids and an old goat.

Zetterberg, with great speed, deft puckhandling ability, and a quick release on his shot, really blossomed in 2005-06 when he posted career-best numbers, finishing with 39 goals and 85 points. The following season a back injury reduced his playing time and his offence to 68 points, but when he was healthy he was good, very good, and was terrific in the post-season for the Red Wings.

Interestingly, Zetterberg had his number 20 retired by Timra in his honour. When he arrived in Detroit, veteran Luc Robitaille, who wore number 20 everywhere he played had the number, so Zetterberg asked for 40, after wearing 15 in a prospect camp.

Says:

"He can stickhandle in a phone booth and pass the puck through the eye of a needle. He'll be one of the best in the game for the next decade and probably the best-ever 210th pick in the draft."

Jim Hughson

Bet You Forgot

Darren Pang wore No. 40 in honour of his childhood hero, Rogie Vachon. "When he went from Los Angeles to Detroit, he donned the number 40," said Pang. "However, in Chicago Jim Ralph had 40 in training camp, so when Ralphie was let go, I asked to wear No. 40." Of note, New York Rangers goalie Stephen Valiquette wears No. 40 in honour of Pang. He has always been a keen admirer of Pang. Fred Brathwaite also wore 40 for a similar reason, although Brathwaite also went to the same high school that Pang did in Nepean, Ontario.

No. 40

1. **Henrik Zetterberg**, Detroit Red Wings
2. **Alex Tanguay**, Colorado Avalanche
3. **Bill Ranford**, Detroit Red Wings
4. **Steve Konowalchuk**, Washington Capitals
5. **Vinny Prospal**, Anaheim Ducks
6. **Mike Rathje**, San Jose Sharks
7. **Patrick Lalime**, Ottawa Senators
8. **Marek Svatos**, Colorado Avalanche
9. **Karlis Skrastins**, Nashville Predators
10. **Darren Pang**, Chicago Blackhawks

Alex Tanguay

Darren Pang

Stu Barnes

If Stu Barnes had decided early in life to wear sweater number 25, it would have been understandable.

He was born on the 25th day of the 12th month in 1970. Yes, he was a Christmas baby.

But Barnes, who was drafted fourth overall by the Winnipeg Jets in 1989, always liked the number four.

"I started wearing number four when I was young for Bobby Orr," says Barnes. "He was the first player that meant a lot to me and I watched him a lot on TV. As you get older, you just end up wearing a higher number when you are a forward. I picked 14 and I've been lucky that almost everywhere I have gone, no one had 14."

Indeed, throughout his career Barnes wore 14. After a couple of seasons in Winnipeg, he was traded to Florida on November 25 (there's that number again), 1993. A few seasons later he was part of the Panthers team that went to the Stanley Cup final, losing in four games to Colorado in 1996. The following season, he was traded to Pittsburgh where he remained for three seasons. He was traded to Buffalo in the spring of 1999 and went to the Cup final that year only to lose to Dallas in six games.

"In Buffalo, I couldn't wear number 14 anymore because it was retired [in honour of French Connection winger Rene Robert]," said Barnes. "So I decided to just exchange the numbers and wore 41 instead."

When he was traded to Dallas a few seasons later, Barnes switched back to 14.

"Stu Barnes is a competitive little guy who made it as a little guy when a lot of little guys didn't, before the NHL made its changes. A real smart forechecker and a real quick skater. I don't know how fast he is but he can go in one direction and then the other direction with a little two-step quickness that gets him away from a lot of big defencemen. He's from the old school and has played on some pretty good hockey teams."

Matt Stajan

No. 41

1. **Stu Barnes**, Buffalo Sabres
2. **Jason Allison**, Boston Bruins
3. **Ray Whitney**, Detroit Red Wings
4. **Brent Gilchrist**, Detroit Red Wings
5. **Jocelyn Thibault**, Quebec Nordiques/Colorado Avalanche
6. **Martin Skoula**, Colorado Avalanche
7. **Dave Hannan**, Buffalo Sabres
8. **Valtteri Filppula**, Detroit Red Wings
9. **Nolan Pratt**, Carolina Hurricanes
10. **Allen Pederson**, Boston Bruins

Brent Gilchrist

Bet You Forgot

A hometown boy, having grown up in Mississauga, a suburb of Toronto, Matt Stajan wore No. 41 in his one appearance with the Maple Leafs in the 2002-03 season. His preferred No. 14 was being worn by Jonas Hoglund. The following season, with Hoglund in Europe, Stajan reversed the digits to 14, honouring both Leafs legend Dave Keon and Stajan's father, a huge Keon fan.

Jason Allison

Sergei Makarov

Sergei Makarov had a lasting impact on the National Hockey League.

He was the oldest rookie to win the Calder Trophy and helped force a rule change as a result.

Makarov, a talented right winger who earned international acclaim playing on a line for the old Soviet Union and 11 seasons with CSKA Moscow with Igor Larionov and Vladimir Krutov, forming the famed KLM line, joined the Calgary Flames in the summer of 1989 at the age of 31. His first season with the Flames, he scored 24 goals and 62 assists to win the Calder. Afterwards, the league lowered the age of eligibility.

Internationally, he was part of two world junior and seven world championship-winning teams. He was also part of a Canada Cup-winning team and twice won Olympic gold.

Makarov, who was good but not great with Calgary, played four seasons with the Flames before moving to San Jose, where he was reunited with Larionov. He made a brief pit stop in Dallas in 1996 before returning to Russia.

In Russia and with the national team, Makarov wore number 24, but when he got to Calgary that number belonged to long-time Flames winger Jim Peplinski, who was a former co-captain. So Makarov flipped the numbers.

"That was his choice," says former Flames general manager Cliff Fletcher. "We told him he couldn't have 24 because Pep had played his whole career there and was a co-captain. He didn't seem to care about it and just decided to flip the numbers."

When he got to San Jose, Makarov got his 24 back, but wore 42 for his four games in Dallas because 24 belonged to Richard Matvichuk.

No. 42

1. **Sergei Markarov**, Calgary Flames
2. **Jon Klemm**, Chicago Blackhawks
3. **Richard Smehlik**, Buffalo Sabres
4. **Kevyn Adams**, Columbus Blue Jackets
5. **Darcy Tucker**, Montreal Canadiens
6. **Kyle Wellwood**, Toronto Maple Leafs
7. **Robert Esche**, Philadelphia Flyers
8. **Tom Preissing**, Ottawa Senators
9. **Mikko Makela**, Boston Bruins
10. **Josef Beranek**, Edmonton Oilers

Richard Smehlik

Kyle Wellwood

Says:

"The KLM line was the best in hockey for a ten-year period. We used to flock to see them practise when they came to North America. His best years were with the Red Army. He'd pretty much retired by the time we saw him in the NHL."

Jim Hughson

Bet You Forgot

The stardom he enjoys now in Toronto was not assured after the Montreal Canadiens chose Darcy Tucker in the 6th round, 151st overall, in the 1993 Entry Draft. Tucker was assigned the rather ignominious No. 42 and put up similarly unglamourous numbers, topping out at seven goals and 20 points in 73 games in the 1996–97 season. The following season, Tucker switched to No. 12 and was dealt to Tampa Bay where he switched to No. 16, the number he wore as a junior with the Kamloops Blazers. Tucker kept the number when he was traded to the Maple Leafs in 2000.

Martin Biron

You could forgive Martin Biron if he felt picked on. He doesn't, but he could have felt that way.

Once upon a time, when he was starting out with the Buffalo Sabres, Biron wore the sweater number 00. But the league, in 1998, ruled that players could no longer wear 0 or 00, so the young goaltender was forced to change from a number he first started wearing in his junior days.

"When I was 16, I played midget AAA in Amos [about four hours north of Montreal]," explains Biron, a native of Lac-St-Charles, Quebec, who was the Sabres' second choice, 16th overall in 1995. "They had some weird numbers to pick from and the goalies had a choice between 00 and 30. The other guy picked 30, so I was left with 00. I had a great year.

"The guys in Beauport let me wear that number again, which was great because I felt like it was something special. The next year, I played my first NHL game with Buffalo at Pittsburgh and the Sabres let me wear 00. Everything seemed to click with that number. Then, one of my childhood friends said to me that he felt there was more to the number. My last name, Biron, could also mean 'Bi' which means 'two' and 'ron' which sounds like 'round' or circle in French. His conclusion was that 'Biron' could be 'two circles.' That was cool. It was even more special.

"Another thing is that every time I had to wear a different number, it seems that I never performed all that good. Then the league made that rule that 00 was not going to be on any jersey any more. I still don't know why, but I had to change my number and I was a little bit worried. Jim Pizzutelli [the Sabres' athletic trainer] and I sat down to look at numbers. Dominik Hasek had 39, so Rip Simonick [Buffalo's equipment manager] suggested I picked 93. I said 'No way.' Curtis Brown was wearing 37, and 34 belonged to Jean-Luc Grand-Pierre, two numbers that I really liked. My brother had 34 in Shawinigan (QMJHL). So I decided to flip it and that's how I got my number.

"The only problem was that Maxim Afinogenov was tagged with that number on the prospects roster. I had more seniority so I stole it from him. Anyway, 61 works better for him.

"That next year was my breakout year with 43. I was an AHL all-star, got my first NHL win, was goalie of the year [in the AHL]. We lost in the Calder Cup Final but it was a great year. I also won a gold medal at the world championship wearing 43. It was a good pick and it's been with me eight seasons."

Biron, who had settled into the number-two role in Buffalo, had asked for and received a trade in February 2007. He was moved to Philadelphia, where he later signed a long-term contract with the Flyers.

"The first thing I did when I got traded to Philly was I looked up their roster to see if anybody had number 43," says Biron. "Luckily, I didn't have to bribe anybody for my number."

HOCKEY NIGHT Says:

"Martin Biron is one of the great guys in the sport. He used to live near me in Buffalo and I would see a lot of him. I never met a goaltender with the personality he's got, especially a goaltender who is as good as he is. He played for Buffalo when they had a string of not-so-good teams but he was always one of the top goaltenders and now Philadelphia's got a gem. I don't know if they realize it or not. If you wanted a good interview after you watched him play a good game, he was the guy to go to."

Harry Neale

No. 43

1. **Martin Biron**, Buffalo Sabres
2. **Philippe Boucher**, Dallas Stars
3. **Patrice Brisebois**, Montreal Canadiens
4. **Ray Whitney**, San Jose Sharks
5. **Al Iafrate**, San Jose Sharks
6. **Martin Straka**, New York Islanders
7. **Ron Flockhart**, Philadelphia Flyers
8. **Dennis Ververgaert**, Philadelphia Flyers
9. **Scott Hannan**, San Jose Sharks
10. **Bryan Fogarty**, Quebec Nordiques

Helmut Balderis

Patrice Brisebois

Bet You Forgot

Another of the first wave of Soviet players, 36-year-old Helmut Balderis became the oldest player ever selected at the NHL's entry draft when the Minnesota North Stars took him in the 12th round in 1989. A star with the Soviet teams of the 1980s, Balderis could not duplicate his totals in the NHL and played just 26 games, scoring only nine points.

44 Chris Pronger

Prior to the draft back in 1993, Alexandre Daigle made a comment that has haunted him forever. "No one remembers who was number two," Daigle was quoted as saying about drafts and the importance of being number one.

He, of course, went first to the Ottawa Senators. Chris Pronger went second to the Hartford Whalers. Fourteen years later, Daigle is still remembered—though not exactly for his hallowed career—and no one has forgotten who was number two.

Indeed, all of that was brought up during the 2007 Stanley Cup final when Pronger made the Senators pay for their mistake one more time, his Anaheim Ducks beating them in five games.

Big, strong, nasty; Pronger is all of that. He is also able to play, on average, 30 minutes a night, work the point on power plays, kill penalties, and score goals. In short, he does it all.

Pronger only played two seasons in Hartford before he was obtained by St. Louis. Then-general manager Mike Keenan was intent on landing the big blue-liner and paid a steep price: fan favourite Brendan Shanahan. It was a deal that worked for both teams, but the Blues got exactly what they were hoping for, soon making the youngster their captain. And in the 1999-2000 season, he won both the Norris and Hart Trophies, the first to do that since Bobby Orr in 1972.

Pronger spent nine successful seasons in St. Louis before financial realities forced the Blues to trade him to Edmonton, where he helped lead the Oilers to a seven-game loss in the final in 2006. He asked for and received a trade, this time to Anaheim, where he teamed up with Scott Niedermayer to lead one of the most imposing defences in the league.

In many ways, the 2007 playoffs captured the essence of Pronger: he played a ton of minutes, was a force at both ends of the rink, was second on the team in scoring, was a remarkable plus-10, and was twice suspended. And in the end he won.

Pronger became the latest addition to the Gold Club, a group of just 19 players worldwide who have won the Stanley Cup as well as gold at the Olympics (2002) and world championships (1997).

In his days of playing minor hockey and high school in Dryden, Ontario, Pronger wore number 14. It was just a number he liked. When he got to Stratford, he changed to number 4, but when he got to junior in Peterborough it was taken and he was left with number 6. He even had a licence plate: CHAOS 6. Drafted by Hartford, 4 was taken when he arrived so he took 44 and kept it in St. Louis and Edmonton.

In Anaheim, Rob Niedermayer had 44. Pronger never contemplated asking for the number, but instead tried something new. He took 7, but the next day changed his mind, figuring a single digit on a big guy didn't look right, so he picked 25 in honour of his friend Mark McGwire.

Whatever the number, no one has forgotten who was number 2 in 1993.

Rob Brown

No. 44

1. **Chris Pronger**, Anaheim Ducks
2. **Dave Babych**, Winnipeg Jets
3. **Todd Bertuzzi**, New York Islanders
4. **Stephane Richer**, Montreal Canadiens
5. **Jason Arnott**, Dallas Stars
6. **Sheldon Souray**, Montreal Canadiens
7. **Slava Fetisov**, Detroit Red Wings
8. **Alexei Zhitnik**, Buffalo Sabres
9. **Glen Murray**, Boston Bruins
10. **Rob Niedermayer**, Florida Panthers

Bet You Forgot

Playing alongside a superstar can be like winning the lottery for some players. Take Rob Brown, who racked up 49 goals and 115 points for the Pittsburgh Penguins in 1988-89 as one of Mario Lemieux's wingers. Unfortunately, Brown never came close to those numbers again.

HOCKEY NIGHT

Says:

"His childhood nickname was 'chaos.' Perfect."

Ron MacLean

Stephane Richer

Sheldon Souray

45

Brenden Morrow

The Dallas Stars raised a few eyebrows when they made Brenden Morrow—at age 27— captain prior to the start of the 2006-07 season.

It had more to do with his leadership skills than any failings by former captain Mike Modano, who resigned to allow the change.

"It was a changing-of-the-guard kind of thing," says Modano. "It's the future for [Morrow] and the future for a lot of the guys who are going to be around here."

Indeed, it was only after the reliable, hard-working Morrow agreed to a six-year contract extension that the decision was made to replace the 36-year-old Modano, who remained as an assistant captain. But the Stars saw Morrow as a leader, and a leader for a long while.

"If we only had him for the one year, we wouldn't have done this," Stars general manager Doug Armstrong explained at the time. "With Brenden's age and the commitment he's made to this organization, he's going to be able to pull this team together for a number of years moving forward."

Morrow joined the Stars in 1999 after being drafted 25th overall out of Portland two years earlier. He wore number 45 his first season because it was the number given to him in training camp, but later changed to number 10.

"It was my training camp number and I wasn't about to tell anybody I didn't like it," says Morrow, adding that he changed to 10 because former teammate Brett Hull had told coach Ken Hitchcock he wasn't going to play on the team if Morrow was wearing a number like 45. Hull was joking, but the change was made.

Morrow's favorite number is actually 19, but it is retired in Dallas in honour of the late Bill Masterton, a Minnesota North Stars player who died in 1968 after hitting his head on the ice. Morrow wore 29 in junior with the Portland Winter Hawks, with whom he won a Memorial Cup, because it was the closest to 19, which was otherwise occupied.

Morrow's best season with the Stars was 2005-06 when he had 65 points.

He is also the son-in-law of former Stars teammate and now Montreal coach Guy Carbonneau, having married his daughter Anne-Marie.

WARRENER ASHAM DIONNE AUDETTE KALININ

No. 45

1. **Brenden Morrow**, Dallas Stars
2. **Rhett Warrener**, Florida Panthers
3. **Arron Asham**, Montreal Canadiens
4. **Gilbert Dionne**, Montreal Canadiens
5. **Donald Audette**, Buffalo Sabres
6. **Dmitri Kalinin**, Buffalo Sabres
7. **Steve Heinze**, Boston Bruins
8. **Matt Cullen**, Anaheim Ducks
9. **Brad Ference**, Florida Panthers
10. **Jocelyn Lemieux**, Montreal Canadiens

Hockey Night in Canada Says:

"Brenden Morrow is a player that every guy—every player, every coach, every GM—would love to have on his team. There's never a shift that he takes off. He's got everything you really need in a hockey player. He's got grit, he's certainly got an edge and a toughness to him. He can score goals. He's a leader, obviously. I look at Morrow as one of those players that you love to have on your team and you hate to have against you."

Drew Remenda

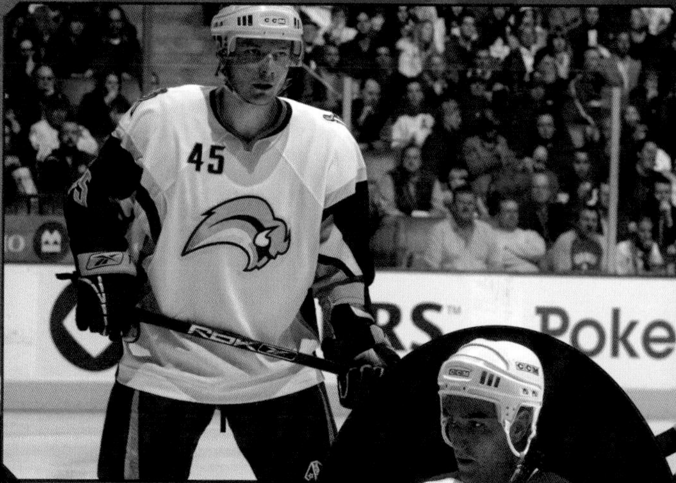

Dmitri Kalinin

Bet You Forgot

While not as accomplished as his older brother when it comes to individual statistics, Gilbert Dionne did one thing his brother Marcel could not manage—he won a Stanley Cup. Wearing No. 45 with the Montreal Canadiens from 1990 to 1995, Gilbert was part of the 1993 Canadiens team that defeated the Los Angeles Kings—Marcel's former team—for the Stanley Cup.

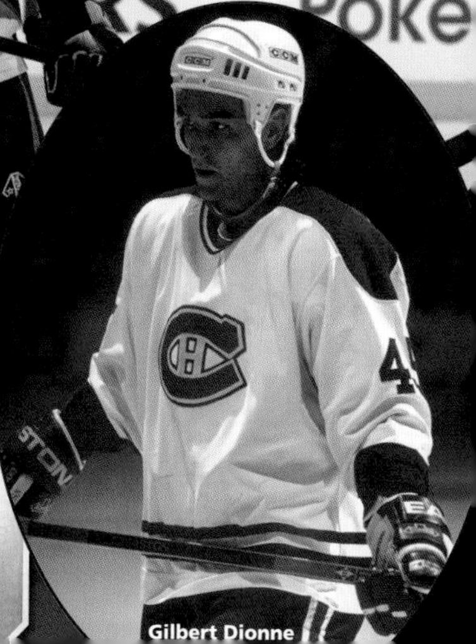

Gilbert Dionne

Martin St. Louis

It's a hoary old saying, but in the case of Martin St. Louis it really is true: sometimes good things really do come in small packages.

At 5-foot-9 and 165 pounds—though he claims he is an inch shorter than listed in his bio—St. Louis was considered by many NHL scouts to be too small to play in the NHL.

After a terrific career at the University of Vermont, where he was a three-time All-American and wore number 8, he went undrafted but was eventually signed by the Calgary Flames as a free agent in 1998, though he was initially dispatched to their farm team in Saint John, New Brunswick.

"I wore 46 [the next fall] in Calgary because that was my training camp number and you couldn't switch until at least November when they knew you had made the team," says St. Louis, who played 13 games in the 1998-99 season for the Flames. "I switched to 15 because it was a more realistic number."

St. Louis wound up splitting another season between Calgary and the minors before he was put on waivers by the Flames. He could have been claimed for just $1 but there were no takers because no team wanted to assume his one-way contract. So, after being bought out by the Flames, he was signed as a free agent by the Tampa Bay Lightning.

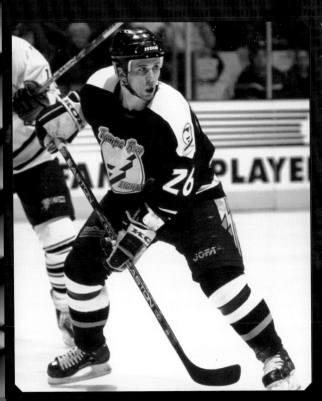

"When I got to Tampa starting over, I switched to my youth hockey number growing up in Laval, which was 26 because my hero was Mats Naslund," says St. Louis of the former diminutive Montreal Canadiens winger.

His first season in Tampa was decent enough and in his second year he was on pace for his best season ever when St. Louis broke his leg. He battled back and in 2003-04 had an unforgettable season, leading the league in scoring with 94 points, winning the Hart and Pearson Trophies, and, most important, the Stanley Cup, beating the Flames in the process in seven games. St. Louis is just the eighth player ever to win all three trophies in the same season.

"He was told no his whole life," says Tampa coach John Tortorella. "But he wouldn't listen."

Sean Pronger

No. 46

1. **Martin St. Louis**, Calgary Flames
2. **Kyle McLaren**, Boston Bruins
3. **Ted Donato**, Boston Bruins
4. **Steve Bernier**, San Jose Sharks
5. **Todd Gill**, Chicago Blackhawks
6. **Andrei Kostitsyn**, Montreal Canadiens
7. **Matt Higgins**, Montreal Canadiens
8. **Curtis Leschyshyn**, Quebec Nordiques
9. **Christian Laflamme**, St. Louis Blues
10. **Sean Pronger**, Boston Bruins

Bet You Forgot

It's not likely Todd Gill, as well as long-suffering Leafs fans, thought the defenceman's career would last 1,000 games after the start he got in the NHL. Thrust on to a woeful Leafs defence in 1984–85, Gill managed to survive the trial by fire and played 12 seasons in Toronto wearing No. 23. After stints in San Jose, St. Louis, Detroit, Phoenix, and Colorado, Gill finished his career with the Chicago Blackhawks in 2002–03 wearing No. 46.

Matt Higgins

"I think he's a guy that had a high skill level who was unsure how to play for a while. I think early on in his career he felt he had to be more of a role player but given an opportunity his high skill level was able to be realized, and I think that's why he's playing like he can in the proper role. He was poorly placed on a team and I think that now that he's in Tampa he's right where he needs to be, playing in a skilled position. He can play at high speed, make plays at high speed, thinks the game real well, and uses his teammates real well."

Kelly Hrudey

Viktor Kozlov

A Valentine's Day baby, Viktor Kozlov felt the love of the San Jose Sharks when the organization drafted him sixth overall in the 1993 Entry Draft.

Born in 1975 in Togliatti, in the former Soviet Union, Kozlov continued to play with the famed Dynamo Moscow team of the Russian league before joining the Sharks in the 1994-95 season, playing 16 games wearing number 47.

At 6-foot-5 and 235 pounds, Kozlov was a dominant presence playing centre and joined the Sharks full-time the following season, switching to number 25 and scoring six goals and 19 points. The next season he improved to 16 goals and 41 points, but was traded to the Florida Panthers on November 13, 1997 and spent the next six years there, his best being 1999-2000 when he had 70 points, including 53 assists.

On March 1, 2004, he was traded to New Jersey, and after playing for his hometown Togliatti Lada during the NHL lockout, he signed with the New York Islanders as a free agent in September 2006. A few months later he became the fifth NHLer to score six goals in consecutive road games, potting two against Pittsburgh on December 2 before exploding for four against the rival New York Rangers on December 3.

Kozlov has had a decent NHL career, but not one befitting a sixth overall pick.

Says:

"One of the most enigmatic Russians. Terrific talent, who shows up once every four or five games, or when there is absolutely no pressure to perform."

Jim Hughson

BERGERON GIGUERE GRAHAME LEBEAU PILON

No. 47

1. **Viktor Kozlov**, San Jose Sharks
2. **Marc-Andre Bergeron**, New York Islanders
3. **Jean-Sebastien Giguere**, Hartford Whalers
4. **John Grahame**, Carolina Hurricanes
5. **Stephan Lebeau**, Montreal Canadiens
6. **Rich Pilon**, New York Islanders
7. **Ladislav Nagy**, St. Louis Blues
8. **Aaron Downey**, Montreal Canadiens
9. **Darren Turcotte**, San Jose Sharks
10. **Claude Lapointe**, Quebec Nordiques

Claude Lapointe

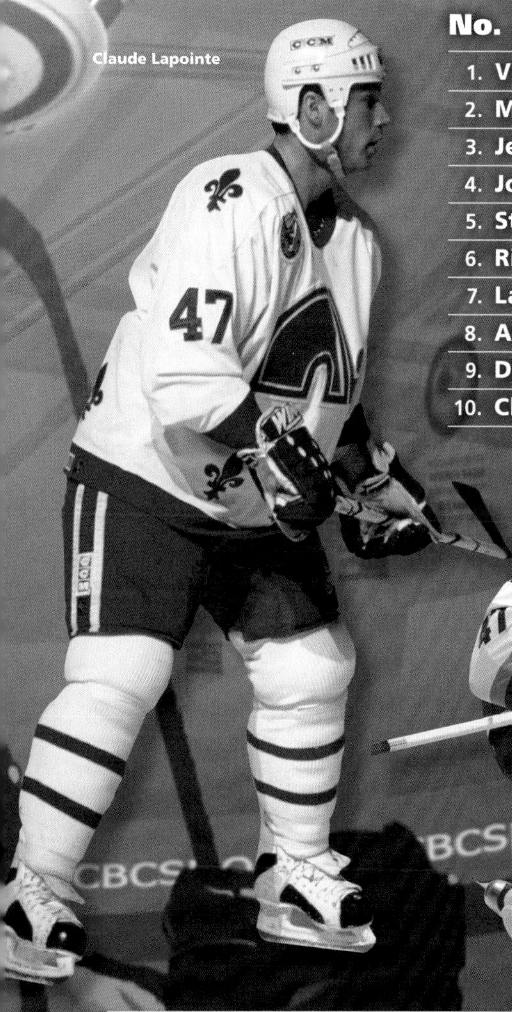

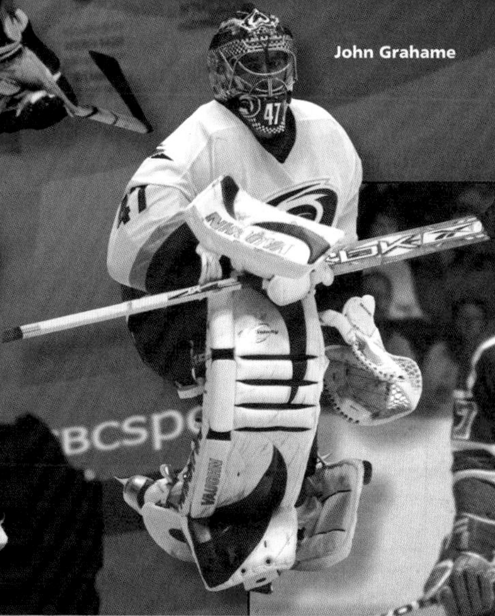

John Grahame

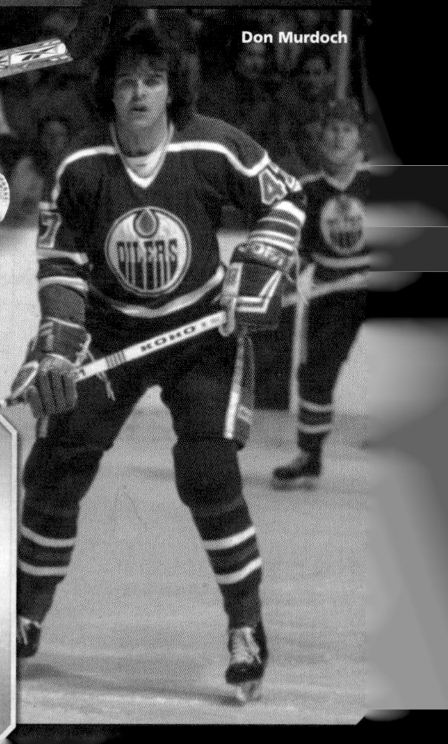

Don Murdoch

Bet You Forgot

On October 12, 1976, a young Don Murdoch was the toast of Broadway after scoring five goals in his New York Rangers' 10-4 win over Minnesota, tying Howie Meeker's record for rookies. Unfortunately, Murdoch never matched his rookie point totals and, after a drug charge and a league suspension, Murdoch found himself in Edmonton, wearing No. 47 and trying to salvage his career. After a number of seasons in the minors, Murdoch retired in 1986.

48

Daniel Briere

Daniel Briere is living proof that good things do sometimes come to those who wait.

Despite his size (just five-foot-10, 170 pounds), Briere has evolved into one of the premiere players in the National Hockey League, a speedster with great playmaking skills.

A first-round pick (24th overall) of the Phoenix Coyotes in 1996, he had consistently been in the 60-point range for four straight seasons, including two with Buffalo, before registering 95 points in 2006-07. Interestingly, that is the same season in which he was awarded a one-year, $5 million contract through salary arbitration.

Briere attended a private high school in Gatineau, where his number 14 was retired, before playing three years of junior with Drummondville in the QMJHL where he was an offensive star. That brilliance really didn't materialize in the NHL until the 2006-07 season, but Briere is definitely a player who has benefited from the new interpretation of the rules in the post-lockout NHL. Last season he was also the most valuable player in the 2006-07 all-star game, his first, finishing with a goal and four assists. He gave the car that came with the award to his sister.

"As a kid I always wore number 8," explains Briere. "I had 14 as a junior in Drummondville. When I started in Phoenix I wanted to wear 14, but it belonged to Mike Stapleton at the time. So I took 8 again. When I was traded to Buffalo, 14 was retired for Rene Robert and my favourite, 8, was taken [by Rory Fitzpatrick]. So I asked to combine the 4 of 14 with 8 to make 48."

Briere, who was an unrestricted free agent, signed a multi-year deal with the Philadelphia Flyers in the summer of 2007.

Says:

"He was on the road to nowhere in Phoenix when a scout who understands small wonders tipped his career. Kevin Devine, Buffalo's head of amateur scouting, is from PEI. He made his home in Phoenix, where he had ample opportunity to catch Coyotes games. He told Darcy Regier, the Sabres' general manager, that Briere was a gem."

Shea Weber

No. 48

1. **Daniel Briere**, Buffalo Sabres
2. **Scott Young**, Quebec Nordiques
3. **Claude Lapointe**, New York Islanders
4. **Andy McDonald**, Anaheim Ducks
5. **Kyle McLaren**, Boston Bruins
6. **Shea Weber**, Nashville Predators
7. **Marcus Nilson**, Florida Panthers
8. **Max Middendorf**, Quebec Nordiques
9. **Darren Van Impe**, Anaheim Ducks
10. **Steve Staios**, Boston Bruins

Scott Young

J.J. Daigneault

Bet You Forgot

Though he got around, playing for 10 teams between 1984 and 2001, J.J. Daigneault is best remembered in Philadelphia. It was with the Flyers that Daigneault scored a last-second goal to win Game 6 of the 1987 Stanley Cup final. Alas, the Oilers prevailed in Game 7, but Daigneault's goal was ranked as one of the Top 10 Flyers moments.

Brian Savage

With an uncle (Larry Hillman) with six Stanley Cups to his credit, Brian Savage might feel regret for not winning one of his own.

However, the Sudbury-born winger does have an Olympic silver medal, won with Canada's national team in the 1994 Winter Olympics.

Taken in the eighth round by Montreal in the 1991 Entry Draft, Savage was still playing with Miami University in Ohio when the Canadiens won their most recent Stanley Cup in 1993. He joined the big club at the end of the 1993-94 season and became a regular two seasons later.

"The Canadiens gave me number 49 at training camp and it was different so I kept it," says Savage, who wore number 17 while in college.

On April 8, 1999, Savage joined Canadiens' legend Joe Malone as the only Habs to record six points in a road game when he had four goals and two assists against the New York Islanders. His best season in Montreal was 1996-97 when he scored 23 goals and added 37 assists and in October 1996 scored the first hat trick in the Bell Centre, the arena that replaced the storied Forum.

Unfortunately, injuries beset much of Savage's career, the worst being cracked vertebrae suffered after being checked into the boards in 1999. He was traded to Phoenix in January 2001 and after two seasons in the desert, was traded to St. Louis late in the 2003-04 season. After the lockout, he signed with Philadelphia for the 2005-06 season and retired in September 2006 having played 674 NHL games and racking up 359 points.

Says:

"It was a career that was hampered too early by injury. I remember when he came to Montreal he looked like he was a real natural goal scorer and he started out and had his good years with the Canadiens. When he was playing well you had the expectation that he might score a goal every time he came on the ice. It's too bad his career ended the way it did."

Dick Irvin

No. 49

1. **Brian Savage**, Montreal Canadiens
2. **Joe Juneau**, Boston Bruins
3. **Matthew Lombardi**, Calgary Flames
4. **Dan Fritsche**, Columbus Blue Jackets
5. **Kip Miller**, Quebec Nordiques
6. **Jon Sim**, Dallas Stars
7. **Vladimir Orszagh**, New York Islanders
8. **Chris Kelly**, Ottawa Senators
9. **Jay Miller**, Los Angeles Kings
10. **Brent Gretzky**, Tampa Bay Lightning

Brent Gretzky

Bet You Forgot
While his brother made No. 99 famous, Brent Gretzky wasn't able to do quite the same for No. 49, which he wore in 13 games with Tampa Bay over two seasons in the early 1990s. Brent, the only one of Gretzky's brothers to make the NHL, recorded one goal and three assists in his career.

Jon Sim

Trevor Letowski

History may one day show that Trevor Letowski had a profound impact on the game of hockey.

It just won't be quite the way he would have preferred, unfortunately.

Letowski, selected 174th overall by Phoenix in 1996, was a high-scoring junior with Sarnia and a member of the 1997 gold-medal winning Canadian world junior team. As a pro, with stops in Vancouver, Columbus and in 2006–07 Carolina, the hard-working winger has been much more defensively oriented. His best NHL season was 1999-2000 with the Coyotes, when he scored a career-high 19 goals and 39 points. But the Thunder Bay native has proven to be a handy player to have around.

As for his impact on the game, well, on October 14, 2006, Letowski was the victim of a blind-side hit from Pittsburgh's Colby Armstrong. He was knocked unconscious, suffered a concussion, and missed nine games as a result. But that incident and several others during the season prompted the league to initiate a crackdown on direct hits to the head, especially those involving a player in a vulnerable position—like Letowski. It's not exactly what a guy wants to be remembered for, but when hits to head are discussed Letowski's name always comes up.

Letowski wore 10 as a junior, but wore number 50 when he debuted with the Coyotes for 14 games in 1998-99. Number 10 was occupied by Oleg Tverdovsky. When he moved on, Letowski claimed the number in Phoenix and wore it in Vancouver and Columbus. With the Hurricanes, however, he wore 19 because 10 is retired in honour of Ron Francis.

Bet You Forgot

Considering 50 is a hallowed number in the NHL when it comes to goal-scoring, it's interesting to note that only two of the 33 players to have worn the number have even reached that total in their career. Trevor Letowski (75) leads the way, followed by Vladimir Orszagh (54).

No. 50

1. **Trevor Letowski**, Phoenix Coyotes
2. **Petr Sykora**, Nashville Predators
3. **Brian Willsie**, Colorado Avalanche
4. **Reinhard Divis**, St. Louis Blues
5. **Dany Sabourin**, Calgary Flames
6. **Eric Fehr**, Washington Capitals
7. **Chris Taylor**, Boston Bruins
8. **Scott Sandelin**, Philadelphia Flyers
9. **Dan Lambert**, Quebec Nordiques
10. **Daniel Berthiaume**, Boston Bruins

51

Brian Campbell

One day, perhaps, a young NHL player will complain that number 51 isn't available because it has been retired, but Brian Campbell has a long way to go to make that happen.

The seventh pick, 156th overall, of the Buffalo Sabres in the 1997 Entry Draft, Campbell wanted to wear number 14 when he arrived in the NHL, but, as he says: "Wherever I go it's been retired," pointing to Peter Lee with the junior Ottawa 67s and Rene Robert with the Sabres.

"I wore 44 in junior instead. [Alexei] Zhitnik had 44 when I got here [to Buffalo]," the 6-foot, 190-pound defenceman says. "They gave me 51 and I've just stuck with it. I'm not a big fan of it, but what are you going to do?"

Campbell, who was born in Strathroy, Ontario, has made the best of it, playing regularly with the Sabres since the 2002-03 season and has seen steady improvement. His best offensive season was 2006-07 when he scored six goals and added 42 assists as the Sabres won the President's Trophy as the top team in the regular season.

Says:

"He came out of Ottawa as a great junior and floundered around for a while as he found his way in the NHL, and now in the past couple of years he has been a good offensive defenceman. He's a good skater and has a nice imagination offensively. He gets in a little trouble defensively on occasion but has really improved, and is one of the reasons Buffalo did so well in 2006–2007."

Harry Neale

No. 51

1. **Brian Campbell**, Buffalo Sabres
2. **Jeremy Roenick**, Chicago Blackhawks
3. **Dave Gagner**, Calgary Flames
4. **Andrei Kovalenko**, Quebec Nordiques
5. **John MacLean**, Dallas Stars
6. **Ryan Getzlaf**, Anaheim Ducks
7. **Francis Bouillon**, Montreal Canadiens
8. **Shawn McEachern**, Los Angeles Kings
9. **Dmitri Mironov**, Detroit Red Wings
10. **Andy Delmore**, Columbus Blue Jackets

Francis Bouillon

Andrei Kovalenko

Jeremy Roenick

Bet You Forgot

It didn't take Jeremy Roenick long to earn a smaller number with the Chicago Blackhawks. After starting his first season in 1988-89 wearing 51, Roenick soon switched to 27, which he would wear for eight seasons in Chicago. The outspoken Roenick stands just five goals shy of 500 after the 2006-07 season and had he reached that plateau, he would have become just the third American player, behind Mike Modano and Joe Mullen, to do it.

Adam Foote

Adam Foote is regarded as being one of the pre-eminent hard-nosed, defensive defencemen in the game—and a winner.

After a good junior career in Sault Ste. Marie, Foote, a native of Whitby, Ontario, was selected 22nd overall by the Quebec Nordiques in 1989. Foote made the team in 1991-92, spending four seasons in Quebec and nine more in Colorado (where the franchise moved), twice winning the Stanley Cup with the Avalanche. Folks there will tell you: next to Patrick Roy and Joe Sakic, Foote was every bit as vital to their success.

Foote, whose career best is 31 points, signed with Columbus as a free agent in the summer of 2005. He has three times played for Canada in the Winter Olympics, winning gold in 2004, and was on two World Cup of Hockey teams.

When Foote played midget hockey in Whitby he wore the number 2. When he played for Sault Ste. Marie in the OHL he wore 5.

"In Nordiques camp [1991] they gave me 52," Foote says.

Of course in those days, quite often the higher the number, the less chance a player was believed to have had to make the team. Well, Foote shocked most by having a very strong camp, but was still one of the final cuts. Pierre Page, the coach and general manager at the time, sent him to Halifax to the AHL where Foote wore the number 25. After six games in the AHL, Page recalled him.

When he returned to the Nordiques, Foote was going to wear number 2 because of his Whitby ties and because Alexei Gusarov had 5 and Stephane Morin had 25. But his Dad, Vern, a long-time Toronto police officer, convinced him to keep 52, because the numbers 5 and 2 had always brought him good luck everywhere he played and because no one, with any regularity, was wearing 52 in the NHL at the time.

"My Dad was my hero," says Foote. "It turned out to be a pretty good choice."

Says:

"In the dictionary, next to 'stay-at-home defenceman,' they should have his name and picture. He blocks shots, he'll do anything to stop a shot. He's a real meat and potatoes guy. Every coach in the league would love to have him on their team."

Dave Andreychuk

No. 52

1. **Adam Foote**, Colorado Avalanche
2. **Dave Andreychuk**, Buffalo Sabres
3. **Craig Rivet**, Montreal Canadiens
4. **Dave Lewis**, Detroit Red Wings
5. **Cam Russell**, Chicago Blackhawks
6. **Alexander Karpovtsev**, Toronto Maple Leafs
7. **Jim Sandlak**, Hartford Whalers
8. **Jason Doig**, Winnipeg Jets
9. **Mike Green**, Washington Capitals
10. **Sven Butenschon**, New York Islanders

Dave Lewis

Alexander Karpovtsev

Bet You Forgot

Dave Lewis just missed his Stanley Cup as a player, but he has won more than a few as a coach. Lewis was one of the players the New York Islanders sent to Los Angeles for Butch Goring in 1980 just before they won four consecutive Stanley Cups. But Lewis persevered and after finishing his career as No. 52 on the Red Wings blue line, he found himself as Scotty Bowman's assistant as the Red Wings won three Stanley Cups between 1997 and 2002.

Nikolai Khabibulin

The "Bulin Wall" proved too high to climb for the Calgary Flames in the 2004 Stanley Cup final, as Nikolai Khabibulin backstopped his Tampa Bay Lightning to a Stanley Cup championship, becoming the first Russian goaltender to win the coveted trophy in the process.

Khabibulin comes by his nickname honestly, having a goals-against average below 3.00 in eight of his 11 seasons. A ninth-round selection of the Winnipeg Jets in the 1992 Entry Draft, Khabibulin moved with the franchise to Phoenix in 1996, playing the next three seasons with the Coyotes and winning at least 30 games in each before a bitter contract dispute in 1999 saw him spend the year in the International Hockey League. He was eventually traded to Tampa Bay and quickly became the team's key ingredient in its Stanley Cup quest.

A free agent following the championship, he signed with Chicago, and with his number 35 retired in honour of Tony Esposito, he reversed the digits to sport 53. He switched to number 39 for the 2006-07 season because it was as close as he could get to 35.

Khabibulin's Stanley Cup wasn't his first championship. In 1992 he was the backup goaltender on the CIS—or former Soviet Union—Olympic team that won gold. Because coaches aren't awarded medals, legendary coach Viktor Tikhonov decided to keep the medal that was supposed to go to Khabibulin and in protest, the goaltender refused to play for Russia at international events for the next 10 years, returning for the 2002 Olympics in Salt Lake City.

Says:

"Everybody knows he helped Tampa Bay win a Stanley Cup, and he was probably the reason that Tampa Bay went into the tank the very next year [after he left to play with the Chicago Blackhawks]. He wasn't given credit for being one of the best goaltenders from the Soviet Union."

Bob Cole

MORRIS CHARA MCLEAN LINDSAY BAKER

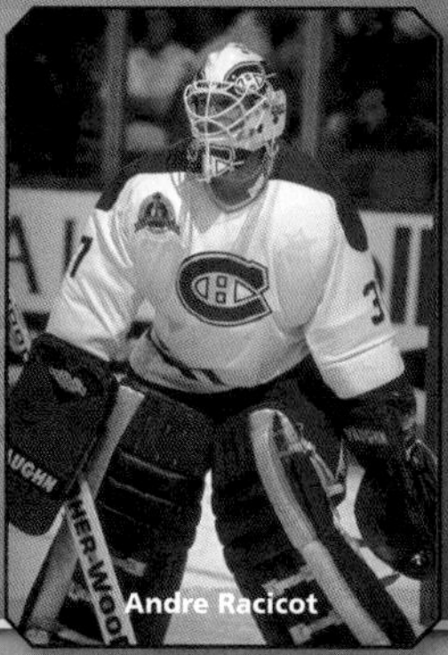

Andre Racicot

No. 53

1. **Nikolai Khabibulin**, Chicago Blackhawks
2. **Derek Morris**, Calgary Flames
3. **Zdeno Chara**, New York Islanders
4. **Brett McLean**, Colorado Avalanche
5. **Bill Lindsay**, Quebec Noridques
6. **Jamie Baker**, Quebec Nordiques
7. **Rory Fitzpatrick**, Montreal Canadiens
8. **Andre Racicot**, Montreal Canadiens
9. **Jason Bowen**, Philadelphia Flyers
10. **Sylvain Blouin**, Montreal Canadiens

Bet You Forgot

Though Andre Racicot's career might be forgettable, his nickname was not. Fairly or unfairly, he was tagged with the moniker "Red Light" for his penchant for letting in bad goals. He played for Montreal from 1989-93 and was Patrick Roy's backup uring the Canadiens' Stanley Cup championship in 1993.

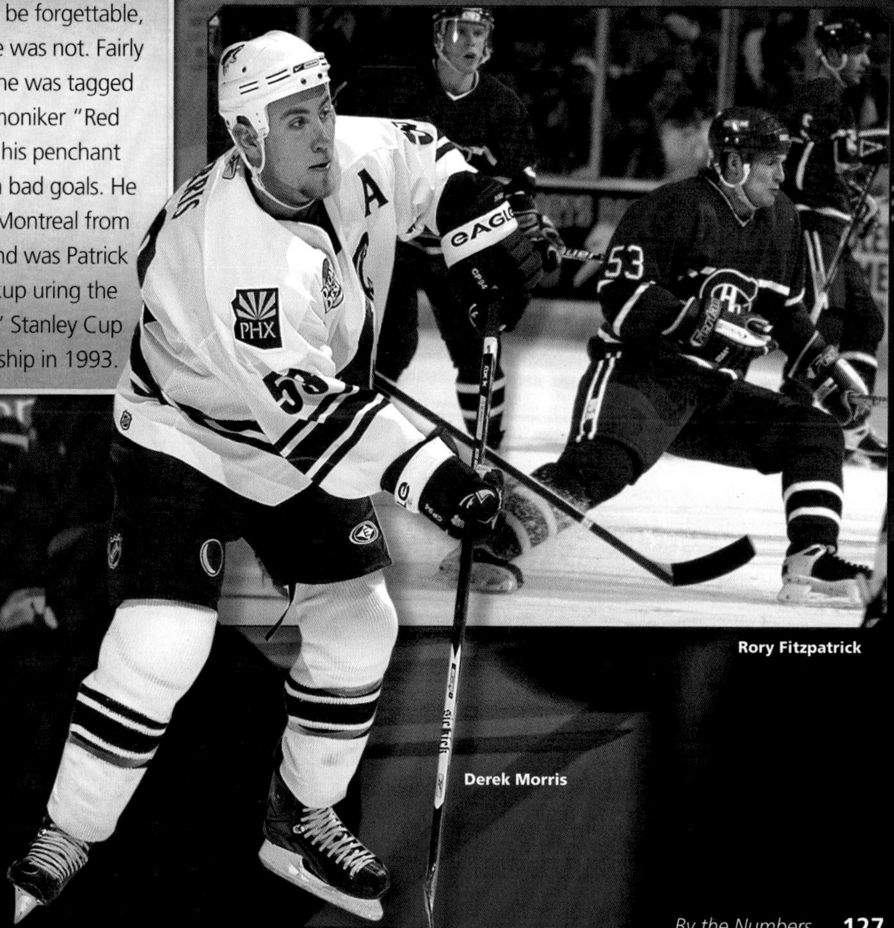

Rory Fitzpatrick

Derek Morris

Hannu Toivonen

Athletes are always acknowledging their mothers with a "Hi mom" if captured on TV, but fathers also play a big part in their success and Hannu Toivonen made sure his was recognized.

The Finnish goaltender, Boston's first-round pick in the 2002 Entry Draft, chose to wear number 54 in honour of his father Harri's birth year of 1954. Recognizing the time, the sacrifices, and the incredible expense of raising a hockey player, Toivonen told *Sports Illustrated*, "I can't thank my parents enough. Hockey's not cheap."

Success in the NHL will help pay them back, as well. Not just in a monetary sense, either.

After a couple of seasons playing with the Bruins' minor-league affiliate in Providence, Toivonen spent the 2005-06 season with the big club, appearing in 20 games and compiling a 9-5-4 record with a respectable 2.63 goals-against average. He struggled in 2006-07, appearing in just 18 games, shuttling back and forth between Boston and the minors.

He was 3-9-1 with the Bruins, with an inflated 4.23 goals-against average, but was signed to a one-year extension, then traded to St. Louis. Hardly a moment of honour, Toivonen was the goaltender of record when Sidney Crosby scored his first NHL goal.

Interestingly, Toivonen told *Sports Illustrated* that, in honour of his mother, Riitta, he wore number 57, her birth year, in junior.

Says:

"Hannu is a former first-round draft choice, who gives our club depth in the goaltending position. Our [St. Louis Blues'] scouts feel he has tremendous upside and a bright future in the National Hockey League. He had a high-ankle injury that he's over. His numbers weren't terrific [in 2006-07], but for whatever reason you need to move on. He's coming to a fresh start, but he's not going to be given anything."

John Davidson

No. 54

1. **Hannu Toivonen**, Boston Bruins
2. **Daniel Briere**, Phoenix Coyotes
3. **Sean Pronger**, Anaheim Ducks
4. **Patrick Traverse**, Montreal Canadiens
5. **Paul Ranger**, Tampa Bay Lightning
6. **Jason Doig**, Washington Capitals
7. **Ed Ward**, Quebec Nordiques
8. **Kip Miller**, New York Islanders
9. **Andre Savage**, Boston Bruins
10. **Kris Newbury**, Toronto Maple Leafs

Daniel Briere

Sean Pronger

Bet You Forgot

These days, Buffalo's Daniel Briere has opposing coaches telling their players to "watch No. 48." But it's not likely coaches took much notice of 54, Briere's number when he began his career in Phoenix in 1997-98. He wore it for just five games before switching to No. 8.

Larry Murphy

As an NHL player, Larry Murphy was around for a long time and, for the most part, a pretty good time.

When he retired after 21 seasons, the native of Scarborough, Ontario, had four Stanley Cup rings and was one of the highest-scoring defencemen in league history. Not bad for a guy who, as a kid, couldn't decide whether to be a forward or a defenceman.

After winning a Memorial Cup with the Peterborough Petes in 1979 and getting to the final again, Murphy was drafted fourth overall by the Los Angeles Kings in 1980. In his rookie season, Murphy impressed immediately, finishing with 60 assists and 76 points, both records for rookie defencemen; he was second in Calder Trophy voting.

He was traded early in his fourth season to Washington in exchange for Ken Houston and Brian Engblom.

His next stop was Minnesota, part of another big trade, where he spent a few seasons before being dealt to Pittsburgh, where he won his first two Stanley Cups in 1991 and 1992. After a few all-star-calibre seasons, Murphy was moved to the Toronto Maple Leafs in the summer of 1995, but the return home was not a good one. The Leafs struggled and the fans made Murphy their favourite whipping boy. He was eventually traded to Detroit prior to the playoffs and helped the Red Wings win back-to-back Cups in 1997 and 1998.

He retired in 2001 with 287 goals and 1,216 points, among the career leaders for defencemen in assists, points, and games played. He had five 20-plus goal seasons and 11 seasons in which he scored 60-plus points. Murphy also won a couple of Canada Cup championships with Team Canada and was the famous decoy on Mario Lemieux's tournament-winning goal in 1987.

"I always liked the number 5, but for no real reason," says Murphy. "I just liked that number. In my mind, defencemen wore single-digit, low numbers. In junior in Peterborough I wore number 2 because 5 wasn't available, but when I got to L.A. that's what they gave me and I was happy with that. But it wasn't a big deal either way.

"In Washington, 5 wasn't available, Rod Langway had it. I only had a couple of options and 8 was the best of a bad lot. I didn't like it, but I didn't dwell on it, either. It wasn't that big a deal. When I went to Minnesota, they stuck me with 8 without talking about it.

"In Pittsburgh, 5 wasn't available (Ulf Samuelsson wore it) but at that point guys were wearing double numbers, so I went with 55 and I had it the rest of the way. The number wasn't a big deal with me, but I just liked the number 5."

Interestingly, in Pittsburgh Murphy often played alongside number 5, Samuelsson. In Detroit, he was often paired with number 5 Nicklas Lidstrom.

Murphy was inducted into the Hockey Hall of Fame in 2004.

No. 55

1. **Larry Murphy**, Pittsburgh Penguins
2. **Sergei Gonchar**, Washington Capitals
3. **Ed Jovanovski**, Vancouver Canucks
4. **Keith Primeau**, Detroit Red Wings
5. **Rob Ramage**, Calgary Flames
6. **Reed Larson**, Buffalo Sabres
7. **Darryl Sydor**, Tampa Bay Lightning
8. **Jason Blake**, New York Islanders
9. **Ulf Samuelsson**, Philadelphia Flyers
10. **Eric Daze**, Chicago Blackhawks

Rob Ramage

Says:

*"He was a like a Saint Bernard.
He wasn't a quick guy—he was a
big, burly guy—but his hockey sense
and his hand-eye coordination was
absolutely outstanding and certainly
a player I really respected when
I played with him."*

Garry Galley

Dave Williams

Bet You Forgot

Dave "Tiger" Williams might have had an inkling about his tenure
with the Detroit Red Wings when he joined the team in 1984-85.
Having worn No. 22 for his entire career, Williams found himself
sporting No. 55 as a Red Wing. Exactly 55 games later, he was
traded to Los Angeles, where he went back to wearing No. 22.

56

Sergei Zubov

For defenceman Sergei Zubov, bad things come in threes.

Having worn number 21 for three seasons with the New York Rangers, including their Stanley Cup championship in 1994, Zubov found the number unavailable after he was traded to the Pittsburgh Penguins on August 31, 1995. Number 21 is retired in Pittsburgh in honour of Michel Brier, a promising prospect who died after a car accident in the early 1970s. So Zubov took number 3. "I played two games and broke my finger," says Zubov, who was the New York Rangers' sixth pick, 85th overall in the 1990 entry draft. "I came back, played one game, broke another finger. So, that was it. There were numbers available with sixes in them, 36, 46, and 56. So I just took the highest number."

Zubov played just that one season in Pittsburgh, recording 11 goals and 66 points, before being traded to Dallas the following June. He continued with both his number 56 and his strong play, helping the Stars win the Stanley Cup in 1999 and playing in the NHL's All-Star Game in 1998, 1999, and 2000.

In 14 NHL seasons, the Moscow-born Zubov has played in more than 1,000 games, totalling 148 goals and 732 points. He is the only active NHL defenceman to record 10 consecutive seasons of 40 or more points, finishing 2006-07 with 12 goals and 42 assists.

Says:

"Zubov is one of the great European defencemen. A little guy, and even when he was little and everyone else was big in the league, and there weren't the restrictions there are now, he was always a guy who I thought could get his shot through from the point. Some guys can't seem to do it regularly and Zubov has very few shots blocked. If you got out too quickly on him at the point he could make the move and go by you. He reminds me of a guy like Pat Stapleton, a defenceman who's small, but big when he plays."

Greg Millen

No. 56

1. **Sergei Zubov**, Dallas Stars
2. **Stephane Robidas**, Montreal Canadiens
3. **David Wilkie**, Montreal Canadiens
4. **Doug Doull**, Boston Bruins
5. **Lubos Bartecko**, St. Louis Blues
6. **Ken Priestlay**, Buffalo Sabres
7. **Alain Nasreddine**, Montreal Canadiens
8. **Jonathan Aitken**, Chicago Blackhawks
9. **Petr Schastlivy**, Ottawa Senators
10. **Kris Beech**, Nashville Predators

Lubos Bartecko

Bet You Forgot

The price of bouncing between the minors and the NHL is one often can't lay claim to a number. So it was for Ken Priestlay, who played parts of two seasons between 1986 and 1988 wearing No. 12 for the Sabres before being forced to switch to 56 when called up in the 1988-89 season.

Steve Heinze

The Boston Bruins considered the request a bit too saucy, but when Steve Heinze was traded to Columbus he finally got his wish. Heinze was finally allowed to wear number 57. So he was Heinze 57, not to be confused with Heinz 57 steak sauce.

Heinze, who wore 23 in Boston, kept the number 57 in stints with both Buffalo and Los Angeles.

Born in Lawrence, Massachusetts, Heinze was chosen in the third round of the 1988 Entry Draft by his home-state Bruins. He would play nine seasons in the black and gold, his best season being 1997-98 when he had 26 goals and 20 assists. He was claimed by Columbus in the 2000 Expansion Draft and played 65 games for the Blue Jackets before being traded to Buffalo.

Heinze finished the season with the Sabres and signed with Los Angeles that summer as an unrestricted free agent. His last season in the NHL was 2002-03, when he had 12 points in 27 games with the Kings.

Says:

"When I played against him, you knew he was the kind of guy who was going to dog the puck all the time. He was always going to be a hard-working guy. You knew you were going to have to be at your best to come out with the puck. He was a kind of guy who was playing in the league because of his work ethic and his ability to battle for pucks like he did."

Garry Galley

Chris Murray

No. 57

1. **Steve Heinze**, Columbus Blue Jackets
2. **Dainius Zubrus**, Montreal Canadiens
3. **P.J. Axelsson**, Boston Bruins
4. **Steve Begin**, Calgary Flames
5. **Garth Murray**, Montreal Canadiens
6. **Chris Murray**, Montreal Canadiens
7. **Antti Laaksonen**, Boston Bruins
8. **George Parros**, Los Angeles Kings
9. **Shawn Heins**, Pittsburgh Penguins
10. **Chris Ferraro**, Pittsburgh Penguins

Chris Ferraro

Bet You Forgot

Dainius Zubrus didn't wear No. 57 long, but he's pretty sure his one appearance wearing it was captured for posterity. After being traded to Montreal from Philadelphia, where he wore No. 9, in March, 1999, the winger was assigned No. 57 with the Canadiens. "For whatever reason they gave me that number and I think there's actually a hockey card to prove it, which I think makes it funny. But there's absolutely no association with that number at all."

Bill Berg

Bill Berg was one of those players every team needed. He wasn't a star, but he was a key contributor.

Noted for his strong defensive play, the native of Beamsville, Ontario, was a hard-working winger who brought energy to the game, checked with enthusiasm, and always battled hard.

Berg, a graduate of the Toronto Marlboros, was a third-round pick, 59th overall, of the New York Islanders in 1986. After a few seasons in the minors, Berg was finally called up by the Islanders in the 1988-89 season, in which he played seven games.

"Mike Walsh, Tom Fitzgerald and I were all called up together," says Berg. "Mike was 53, I was 58, and Fitzy was 59. We called ourselves the linebacker crew. Those were our training camp numbers."

The numbers were a definite indication of where the youngsters stood in the pecking order. So, too, were the sweaters they were given when the team photo was taken. All three wore practice jerseys and when the picture was being taken, they were skating at the other end of the rink.

The affable left winger played another full season in the minors before joining the Isles full-time in 1990. That season he wore number 4.

"In Springfield the year before I wore number 4 and we won the Calder Cup," says Berg. "So when I started with the Isles in training camp I thought 4 would be good luck. It wasn't very good luck because we didn't do so well so I thought I would switch numbers. I wanted 10, but it was taken."

So for the next season and the one after he wore 17 until he was claimed on waivers by the Toronto Maple Leafs in December 1992. Berg became a key contributor with the Leafs playing on a checking line with Peter Zezel and Mark Osborne. That season and next the Leafs went to the semifinals and Berg certainly helped the cause.

In Toronto, he wore number 10.

"That was my favourite number, I always wanted it," says Berg.

Berg was eventually traded to the New York Rangers in February 1996 for Nick Kypreos. In New York, he wore 18, the number selected by general manager Neil Smith.

"Didn't have a choice," he says. "They just assigned numbers."

The final stop was Ottawa, acquired by the Senators along with a draft pick for Stan Neckar. There he wore number 9.

"They picked it," says Berg. "There's a lot of pressure wearing a number like 9. I don't know who made that decision, but as soon as I saw that number I said to the trainer, 'I don't know what you guys are expecting.'"

Interestingly, Berg didn't realize that number 10 in Toronto had its own rich history, worn by captain George Armstrong when the Leafs last won the Stanley Cup in 1967.

"I might have considered it a bit more had I known," he says. "But back then I knew more about George Ferguson than George Armstrong."

Berg retired in 1999.

Hockey Night Says:

"Bill Berg was a hard-working guy; not much of a goal scorer but lots of hustle and energy, and a pretty bright player. He played on a line for the Leafs with Peter Zezel and Mark Osborne that was the shutdown line and he chipped in a reasonable number of goals."

Harry Neale

No. 58

1. **Bill Berg**, New York Islanders
2. **Sergei Krivokrasov**, Chicago Blackhawks
3. **Robert Kron**, Vancouver Canucks
4. **Steve Montador**, Calgary Flames
5. **Kris Letang**, Pittsburgh Penguins
6. **Kevin Dallman**, Boston Bruins
7. **Sergei Varlamov**, Calgary Flames
8. **Aris Brimanis**, New York Islanders
9. **Jean-Francois Fortin**, Washington Capitals
10. **Dan Hinote**, St. Louis Blues

Robert Kron

Bill Berg

Bet You Forgot

Players can get creative when they find their usual number unavailable. Take Dan Hinote, who couldn't get No. 13, the number he had worn for six seasons with the Colorado Avalanche, when he signed as a free agent with St. Louis in the summer of 2006. Hinote simply chose No. 58 because added together, the numerals equaled 13.

59 Tom Fitzgerald

Tom Fitzgerald was never a star in the NHL, but he was a good leader and the kind of reliable player teams liked to have around.

This is why he was twice selected in Expansion Drafts: because his skills and his leadership abilities were in demand.

The affable Fitzgerald was selected 17th overall by the New York Islanders in 1986, but was allowed to play two seasons at Providence College before turning pro, starting with the Springfield farm team. That season, he was called up to New York, which is when he wore number 59.

Along with Mike Walsh (53) and Bill Berg (58), Fitzgerald wore 59 as a rookie and the three of them called themselves the linebacker crew, a bunch of young kids with high numbers looking to stick in the NHL.

Over his first four seasons, Fitzgerald split time between the minors and the Islanders, before becoming a full-time NHLer in 1992-93.

"After 59, I switched to 7, no significance, it was the lowest available. But they told me in my third year that it was a defenceman's number, so they gave me 14."

Ironically, after finally cracking the Islanders' lineup, he was left exposed in the Expansion Draft and was selected by the Florida Panthers, which turned out to be a good thing. Fitzgerald played well for the Panthers over five seasons, including a visit to the Stanley Cup finals in 1996.

"I was given my choice of numbers in Florida," says Fitzgerald. "I wore 12 in high school and college, but I wanted a fresh start so I reversed numbers and went with 21."

When Fitzgerald was traded to Colorado for 11 games, "I wanted 21 but some guy named Peter Forsberg had it, so I wore 14, a familiar number." Fitzgerald then found his way to Nashville through the Expansion Draft, where he wore 21.

After four seasons in the Music City, where he became captain, he was moved to Chicago, before signing with Toronto and ultimately Boston as a free agent.

"Chicago had 12 available so I jumped all over it," he says. "Same in Toronto and Boston."

Fitzgerald, a native of Billerica, Massachusetts, was very good defensively—a faceoff specialist—but also had decent offensive skills. After one season in Boston he retired after living out a childhood dream.

"Of course, my favourite number was number four," he says. "My favourite player growing up in Boston was Bobby Orr."

No. 59

1. **Tom Fitzgerald**, New York Islanders
2. **Travis Moen**, Chicago Blackhawks
3. **Robert Dome**, Pittsburgh Penguins
4. **Michel Ouellet**, Pittsburgh Penguins
5. **Chad LaRose**, Carolina Hurricanes
6. **Dave Karpa**, Quebec Nordiques
7. **Alain Nasreddine**, New York Islanders
8. **Rich Brennan**, Boston Bruins
9. **Brian White**, Colorado Avalanche
10. **Jeff Hoggan**, St. Louis Blues

Says:

"Fitzy was the best icer I've ever seen and that means he killed a lot of penalties and he didn't have to have the puck on his stick more than half a second. He had the ability to find the hole and get it down the ice. I know everyone kind of laughed when I said he was the best icer in the NHL but when you look for that, he can do it. A lot of penalty killers do a good job getting in the passing lanes and blocking shots, but somehow when they get the puck, for the split second they have it, they can't find the opening."

Harry Neale

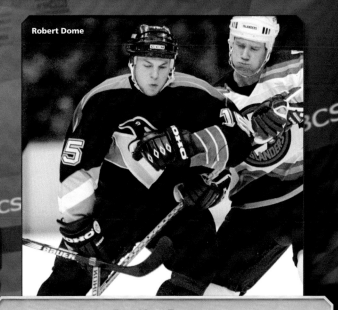

Robert Dome

Bet You Forgot

The Pittsburgh Penguins had high hopes for Robert Dome when he was drafted 17th overall in 1979 out of Las Vegas in the IHL. He was a terrific junior in the Czech Republic, but was never able to really make the transition to the NHL. The centre/left winger played just 53 games with the Penguins, producing 14 points. He was signed by Calgary as a free agent in 2002 and played just one game before heading back to Europe.

Jose Theodore

Jose Theodore's road to his perfect number took a few turns. The Quebec-born goaltender sported number 37 when he first appeared in goal with the Montreal Canadiens in 1995-96, but his tenure in the NHL lasted just nine minutes and he was returned to the Hull Olympiques of the Quebec Major Junior League.

When he returned to the Habs the following season, 37 had been assumed by Tomas Vokoun (who ironically, played just one game that season) so Theodore considered his options.

One idea was to wear number 20 in honour of Soviet great Vladislav Tretiak, whose goalie school Theodore had attended. Alas, Eddie Belfour had settled on that number in San Jose and in search of something unique, according to Habs historian Carl Lavigne, Theodore settled on number 60 after the Canadiens' equipment manager told him he would be the first NHL goalie to wear it.

The Canadiens' second pick in the 1994 Entry Draft, Theodore's potential was fully realized in the 2001-02 season when he won 30 games with a 2.11 goals-against average behind a mediocre Canadiens squad. Theodore was rewarded with both the Vezina Trophy as top goaltender and the Hart Trophy as league MVP. He also helped the Canadiens upset the Bruins in the playoffs in 2002.

Theodore also belongs to a select club of netminders who have scored goals, achieving the feat on January 2, 2001, against the New York Islanders.

In 2006, Theodore, struggling to find his form, was traded to Colorado, where he has enjoyed some good moments with the Avalanche, but has been inconsistent.

Says:

"The year [2002] that he won everything—the Hart and the Vezina and what have you—he deserved every bit of it. I saw a lot of great goaltenders play for the Montreal Canadiens and I don't remember any of them that did as much for the team during the course of one season than he did that year. He got them where they got to and he was very, very worthy of all the awards he got. He played as good that year as I've ever seen a goaltender play during the course of one season. The problem was, I think, that when he signed the big contract following that, he couldn't handle it."

Dick Irvin

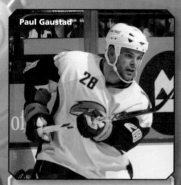

Paul Gaustad

No. 60

1. **Jose Theodore**, Montreal Canadiens
2. **Paul Gaustad**, Buffalo Sabres
3. **Michal Grosek**, Winnipeg Jets
4. **Travis Brigley**, Colorado Avalanche
5. **Brian Finley**, Boston Bruins
6. **Ray Schultz**, New York Islanders
7. **Don Barber,** Quebec Nordiques
8. **Kirk Nielsen**, Boston Bruins
9. **Frederic Cloutier**, New York Islanders
10. **Andy Rymsha**, Quebec Nordiques

Bet You Forgot

Paul Gaustad on why he once wore No. 60 with the Sabres: "Oh gosh, it's only because that's what they gave me. Actually that's always how it's been with all the numbers I've worn, I just take what they give me. I've never really requested a number. In junior when I first got to the Portland Winter-hawks they gave me No. 14 and I was just so excited to be on the team that I would take any number. That's how all of my numbers have evolved. They also gave me No. 14 in the AHL. When I made my NHL debut it was No. 60 and I didn't care what number it was. And then when I made the Sabres (for good) they didn't have No. 14 so they gave me No. 28. So No. 60 was just one NHL game, it was during my first AHL season and I got called up. It was just one game with that number."

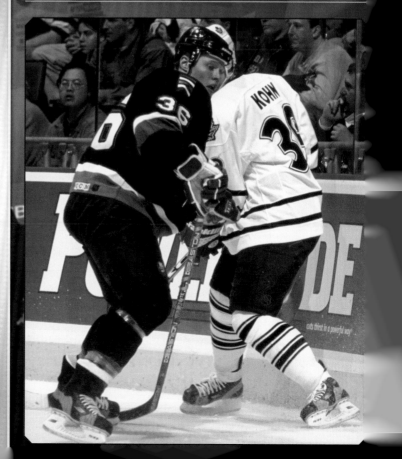

61

Rick Nash

Rick Nash has never been the superstitious type, but others around him certainly have, which is why he is wearing number 61 with the Columbus Blue Jackets instead of his favoured number 13.

It all started in junior hockey with the OHL London Knights.

"I went to London in training camp and the trainer, Don Brankley, asked me what number I wanted," says Nash, who was the first pick overall in the 2002 NHL draft. "I wore 13 coming into the (junior) draft and they didn't allow 13 in London because of the superstition. So I asked for 16 and he said a veteran was already wearing it. At that point I told him, 'I don't care, it doesn't matter to me.'

"The next day I came to the rink and Branks had 61 in my stall and then I just stuck with it. The next year the veteran was gone and he asked me if I wanted 16, but I just thought I'd stick with 61."

Will he always keep it?

"Yeah. It worked for the first season, I had a good year. Because of Don Brankley and the London Knights, that's why I'm 61. I don't think I'll ever change it if I don't have to now."

The only time since then that Nash didn't wear number 61 was in 2002 at the world junior tournament. He had to wear number 38 instead because Hockey Canada wasn't allowing the higher numbers. Nash asked why, at the time, Vicki Sunohara could wear 61 for the national women's team, but he was left with 38.

"It was good, I was young," says Nash. "I didn't see much ice, but it was a great experience. It was a lot of fun."

As a kid growing up in the suburbs of Toronto, Nash wore 13.

"I stuck with 13 for the most part because of [Maple Leafs captain] Mats Sundin. I played [minor hockey] for the Marlies. He was my favourite player growing up, so that was really the only reason I wore 13."

And he clearly wasn't superstitious.

"I thought it was good luck."

Nash's best season with the Blue Jackets was 2003-04 when he scored 41 goals, tying him for the league lead with Jarome Iginla and Ilya Kovalchuk, and giving him a share of the Maurice Richard Trophy.

Injuries abbreviated his 2005-06 season, though he still managed 31 goals in 54 games and was selected to the Canadian Olympic team. Nash had just 27 goals in 2006-07, but did help lead Canada to gold at the world championships in Moscow, where he was named most valuable player.

Sylvain Turgeon

No. 61

1. **Rick Nash**, Columbus Blue Jackets
2. **Cory Stillman**, St. Louis Blues
3. **Maxim Afinogenov**, Buffalo Sabres
4. **Corey Perry**, Anaheim Ducks
5. **Sylvain Turgeon**, Ottawa Senators
6. **Pat Hickey**, St. Louis Blues
7. **Mike York**, Philadelphia Flyers
8. **Alex Selivanov**, Tampa Bay Lightning
9. **Pascal Dupuis**, New York Rangers
10. **Jason Ward**, Montreal Canadiens

Maxim Afinogenov

Says:

"His clinching goal at the 2007 World Championship in Moscow will rank as one of the finest in the history of Canada's participation on the world stage."

Ron MacLean

Bet You Forgot

Players often have interesting stories about how they settled on a jersey number, but if Buffalo's Maxim Afinogenov has one, he's not saying. Asked why he wears No. 61, Aginogenov refused to answer, saying he had his reasons but would not tell why. "It's my reason, I'm not going to tell why. I've pretty much always worn No. 61. On Moscow Dynamo we couldn't wear the big numbers and I switched to 31 for a couple of years."

62 Olli Jokinen

Like a fine wine, Finland-born Olli Jokinen has only gotten better with age.

Drafted with great promise as the third overall pick by the Los Angeles Kings in the 1997 Entry Draft—tied as the highest-drafted Finnish player—the 6-foot-3, 205-pound centre showed little to justify his high ranking and was traded by the Kings to the New York Islanders in June 1999 in a multi-player deal that saw Ziggy Palffy head west. After another tepid season in Long Island, where he scored just 11 goals with 10 assists, he was traded again, this time to Florida along with a young goaltender named Roberto Luongo.

It was in the Florida sunshine where Jokinen really blossomed. Wearing number 12, having worn number 62 with the Isles, Jokinen had 36 goals and 65 points in 2002-03 and was named the team's captain. He followed that up with 26 goals the next season, earning a spot on the Eastern Conference All-Star game roster.

After a year in Europe during the lockout, he came back to the Panthers and racked up 38 goals and 89 points. In 2006-07, with a new four-year, multi-million dollar deal in his pocket, he led the Panthers with 39 goals and 91 points. In February 2006, he helped Team Finland win a silver medal at the Turin Olympics.

His favourite players growing up were former stars Jari Kurri and Esa Tikkanen.

Says:

"Olli Jokinen is a guy that has so much skill—he's got size and a ton of skill—and I don't think a lot of us understand Jokinen's ability because we don't see him an awful lot. He's kind of been obscured by the team [Florida] that he plays for. I look at Jokinen and think this guy probably has everything you really need in a hockey player but his biggest problem is he's not had a surrounding cast that can help break everything out in him. This guy is a complete, high-level skill hockey player.

No. 62

1. **Olli Jokinen**, New York Islanders
2. **Paul Stastny**, Colorado Avalanche
3. **Andrei Nazarov**, Tampa Bay Lightning
4. **Jaroslav Svoboda**, Carolina Hurricanes
5. **Martin Rucinsky**, St. Louis Blues
6. **Rico Fata**, Calgary Flames
7. **Vaclav Nedorost**, Florida Panthers
8. **Steve Webb**, New York Islanders
9. **Duncan Milroy**, Montreal Canadiens
10. **Scott Barne**y, Los Angeles Kings

Paul Stastny

Andrei Nazarov

Steve Webb

Bet You Forgot

Andrei Nazarov changed more than a few minds about the toughness of European players. The 6-foot-5, 242-pound winger, who wore No. 62 with the Calgary Flames for two seasons in the late 1990s, amassed 1,409 penalty minutes in his 11 seasons in

Mike Ribeiro

Mike Ribeiro lived the dream of almost every boy growing up in Montreal when his hometown Canadiens made him their second choice, 45th overall, in the 1998 Entry Draft.

But with that dream comes pressure and it is hard for young players to succeed—especially in Montreal—because of the pressure and expectations.

After bouncing between the big club and its minor-league affiliate, Ribeiro began to show promise in the 2003-04 season when he scored 20 goals and 65 points in 81 games. After spending part of the lockout playing in Finland, the 6-foot centre returned to Montreal with another solid 51-point season but was then traded to the Dallas Stars, where he led the team in scoring in the 2006-07 season with 59 points.

Having worn number 71, his training camp number, in Montreal, Ribeiro was ripe for a change after the move to Dallas and switched to the number 63. The reason, according to the Stars, is that as a kid 9 had always been his favourite number. He had worn the numbers 3, 6, and 9. Do the math: 6 plus 3 equals 9. So he switched to 63 in Dallas. The change, it would seem, has worked nicely.

Says:

"He certainly has a good skill level. I kind of look at Ribeiro as being in-between on a lot of things. He's got good size but he's not very heavy—he's only about 180 pounds, but he's six foot. I think he sees the ice really well and he's really creative with the puck. When he has the puck he tries to make plays. His first instinct isn't to get rid of the puck or dump it in or do the safe thing, what coaches call high percentage hockey. What Ribeiro does offensively, he thinks the game really well and he's got great instincts. I think he's sometimes not strong enough physically defensively to battle one-on-one and win those battles."

No. 63

1. **Mike Ribeiro**, Dallas Stars
2. **Josef Vasicek**, Carolina Hurricanes
3. **Brad Norton**, Los Angeles Kings
4. **Patrick Traverse**, Boston Bruins
5. **Radoslav Suchy**, Phoenix Coyotes
6. **Craig Darby**, Montreal Canadiens
7. **Justin Papineau**, St. Louis Blues
8. **Matt Herr**, Boston Bruins
9. **Cole Jarrett**, New York Islanders
10. **Rene Chapdelaine**, Los Angeles Kings

Bet You Forgot

There's little to distinguish the career of Joel Prpic other than he is one of the taller players to suit up in the NHL. The 6-foot-6 defenceman wore No. 63 for three games with the 2000-01 Colorado Avalanche.

Josef Vasicek

64

Darrin Shannon

It's rare enough for brothers to both play in the NHL and rarer still for them to play on the same team, but Darrin Shannon got that opportunity when he and his older brother Darryl played for the Winnipeg Jets from 1993 to 1996.

Born in Barrie, Ontario, Darrin was the first pick, fourth overall, of the Pittsburgh Penguins in the 1988 Entry Draft. However, he was traded to Buffalo before ever donning a Penguins uniform and played three games for the Sabres in the 1988-89 season. Interestingly, Shannon was packaged with Doug Bodger, with goaltender Tom Barrasso heading to the Penguins, where he later helped lead Pittsburgh to back-to-back Stanley Cup victories.

After playing sparingly for a couple of more seasons, Shannon was traded to Winnipeg in October 1991 and became a regular winger with the Jets. He briefly wore number 64 before switching to 34. His best season came in 1992-93 when he scored 20 goals and 60 points, following that up the next year with 21 goals and 58 points.

However, a knee injury in 1998 effectively ended his career and after stints in the minors with Grand Rapids, St. John's, and Chicago, Darrin retired from hockey in 2000.

"A really hard-working guy. Strong as a physical player. He had pretty good size. Not a bad set of hands, he had a couple of 20-goal seasons with the Jets. He's one of those guys you love in the NHL because he was a guy who every shift would max out. He got the most out of his ability because of his work ethic."

Drew Remenda

Jason Bonsignore

No. 64

1. **Darrin Shannon**, Winnipeg Jets
2. **Jason Bonsignore**, Edmonton Oilers
3. **Wyatt Smith**, Phoenix Coyotes
4. **Jarno Kultanen**, Boston Bruins
5. **Jean-Philippe Côté**, Montreal Canadiens
6. **Armand Mondou**, Montreal Canadiens
7. **Roman Tvrdon**, Washington Capitals
8. **David Moravec**, Buffalo Sabres

Jarno Kultanen

Bet You Forgot

The number 64 proved quite fruitful for Montreal's Armand Mondou in the 1934-35 season, at least in the eyes of the NHL's referees. That was the season penalty shots were introduced and Mondou was awarded three of the first four taken in NHL history, scoring on one.

Mark Napier

Mark Napier was always a great goal scorer.

Gifted with terrific speed and a deft touch, Napier never had a problem finding the back of the net. Just like his two childhood idols, Bobby Hull and Gordie Howe, which is why he always favoured the number 9.

As a junior, playing with the Toronto Marlies and wearing the number 14, Napier was a prolific scorer. In 1975 he led the way with 66 goals in the regular season and another 24 in the playoffs en route to a Memorial Cup championship. The next season, as an 18-year-old, the flashy winger turned pro with the Toronto Toros of the World Hockey Association.

Wearing his lucky number 9, Napier had 43 goals his first season to win rookie-of-the-year honours, and 60 goals the next year, when the team had moved to Birmingham. After three years in the WHA, Napier joined the Montreal Canadiens, who had drafted him 10th overall in 1977. His first season in Montreal he had 31 points as the Canadiens won yet another Stanley Cup.

"In Montreal, I was given 31 and had no choice," says Napier. "In Montreal at the time, you got the next number available. Your only choice was when a number came open."

After five seasons in Montreal, Napier was part of a trade for Bobby Smith with Minnesota. There he wore 16 for no particular reason and was moved the following season to Edmonton.

"I wore 18 there—two nines—but I switched for Danny Gare. When he came to Edmonton I offered him my number because that was the number he wore his whole career. I was searching for a number and chose 65."

At the time, Napier was the honourary chair of the local Cystic Fibrosis Foundation, which had a fundraising campaign called 65 Roses. He changed to 65 to bring attention to the charity.

"I wore 65 the rest of my career," says Napier, who scored 235 goals in the NHL over 11 seasons and won two Cups.

Says:

"He was one of those guys, real good on the second or third line, the guys you need to have. You can't have all stars. He was a solid guy, up and down the ice, never gave you any trouble, and you never had a problem

No. 65

1. **Mark Napier**, Edmonton Oilers
2. **Ron Hainsey**, Montreal Canadiens
3. **Tim Hunter**, Quebec Nordiques
4. **Brett Harkins**, Boston Bruins
5. **Chris Conner**, Dallas Stars
6. **Nathan Guenin**, Philadelphia Flyers

Ron Hainsey

Tim Hunter

Bet You Forgot

After wearing No. 19 for 11 seasons with Calgary, rugged forward Tim Hunter wound up in Quebec after being claimed by Tampa Bay in the 1992 expansion draft. He wore 65 for just 48 games before being traded to Vancouver later that season. The 65 was because of his involvement with the Cystic Fibrosis charity 65 Roses.

Brett Harkins

Mario Lemieux

With his play in junior hockey already inviting comparisons to Wayne Gretzky, Mario Lemieux's agent turned the expectations up considerably when he suggested the next one wear number 66.

The reason? It was 99 upside down. That Lemieux's agent, Gus Badali, was also Gretzky's agent

didn't make the move any less precocious, but from his first shift in his first NHL game, when he scored his first goal, Lemieux showed he was up to the challenge.

Lemieux's remarkable career would wind up 20 years later with 690 goals and 1,723 points and innumerable trophies and awards. He won the Art Ross Trophy six times, his best season being 1988-89, when he had 85 goals and 199 points. He was awarded the Hart Trophy in 1988, 1993, and 1996 and when the Penguins won back-to-back Stanley Cups in 1991 and 1992 he was the Conn Smythe Trophy winner both times.

But perhaps even more remarkable than those accolades was Lemieux's battle with injuries and poor health, none more serious than the Hodgkin's disease he was diagnosed with in January 1993. Lemieux was in the midst of a stellar offensive season, but was forced to miss a month as he underwent treatment to fight the cancer.

When he returned, he was 12 points back of Buffalo centre Pat Lafontaine in the points race, but Lemieux went on a tear, scoring 30 goals and 26 assists in 20 games to overtake Lafontaine and win his fourth Art Ross Trophy.

Though the cancer was beaten, Lemieux continued to be dogged by back injuries and following the 1996-97 season he retired, and was immediately inducted into the Hockey Hall of Fame.

The game, though, pulled him back when the Penguins' financial difficulties threatened Lemieux's deferred salary, and in 1999 Lemieux bought the franchise. Knowing his presence would enhance the team's financial and hockey prospects, Lemieux ended his retirement and on December 27, 2000, returned to the ice against the Toronto Maple Leafs, scoring a goal and two assists in his first NHL game in four years.

In 2002, Lemieux was captain of the Canadian hockey team that won the country's first hockey gold medal in 50 years, and it's fitting that Gretzky was the general manager. He will also always be remembered for his Canada Cup-winning goal in 1987, set up by Gretzky. As a junior, before switching to 66, Lemieux wore 27 after his brother Alain.

 Says: "None finer than Mario Lemieux. He had the most finesse of any hockey player. He looked not as fast as he really was and nobody excited me any better or more often than Mario. He was in a class by himself."

Bob Cole

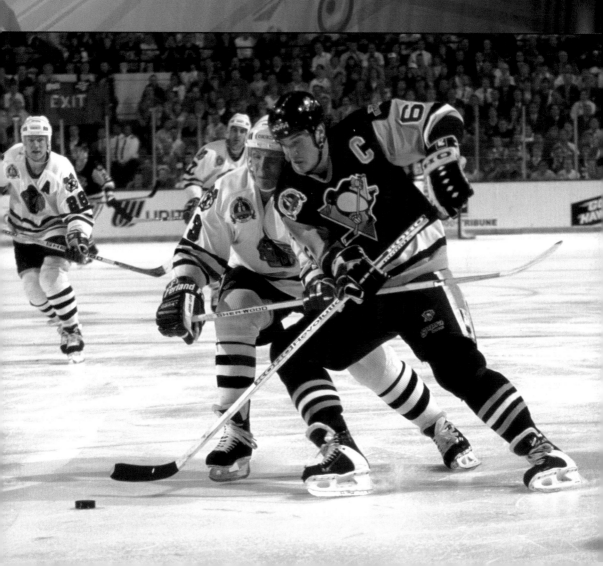

66

ODJICK DUPRE NOVY

No. 66

1. **Mario Lemieux**,
   Pittsburgh Penguins

2. **Gino Odjick**,
   Vancouver Canucks

3. **Yanick Dupre**,
   Philadelphia Flyers

4. **Milan Novy**,
   Washington Capitals

Mario Lemieux

Gino Odjick

DUPRE

ODJICK

NOVY

Milan Novy

Yanick Dupre

Bet You Forgot

A star for the Czech national team in the 1970s, Milan Novy
played one season in the NHL with the Washington Capitals. His
usual number was No. 6 but it was already taken. He tried 26 and

67

Robert Svehla

The number 67 isn't a very popular one in Toronto and that isn't entirely the fault of Robert Svehla.

It is mostly to do with the year 1967: the last year the Maple Leafs won the Stanley Cup. Forty years later, Leafs fans are still waiting for a repeat and getting more frustrated with each passing season.

In the one season Svehla played in Toronto—2002-03—he wore that number. Throughout his career he had worn 24, but when he was signed by the Leafs, who had to entice him out of a premature 35-day retirement with a sweetened contract and trade with Florida for his services, Bryan McCabe was wearing his favoured number.

So he chose 67.

"I signed him," says former Leafs assistant general manager Bill Watters. "As I recall, he took a fair bit of heat for picking the number. People thought he was poking fun at the last Cup year, but I don't think he was. He wasn't that kind of kid. I think he was simply acknowledging it and that was it."

Whatever the motive, Svehla at times wasn't popular with Leafs management because of his ongoing contract issues. After his one season, in which he actually played quite well, the Leafs exercised an option to bring him back. But this time Svehla retired for good from the NHL after nine seasons, leaving the Leafs short on quality defencemen.

Originally drafted by Calgary, he spent eight seasons with the Florida Panthers, including their run to the Stanley Cup final.

Svehla is from Martin, Slovakia and was a part owner of his former club team, Dukla Trencin.

"A quiet kind of player but I think he really played some good hockey. He's not a flashy kind of player, he doesn't do anything particularly outstanding, but he does a lot of things

No. 67

1. **Robert Svehla**, Toronto Maple Leafs
2. **Benoit Pouliot**, Minnesota Wild
3. **Mike Kennedy**, New York Islanders
4. **Tom Askey**, Anaheim Ducks

Bet You Forgot

Like so many youngsters, one of the biggest influences in Benoit Pouliot's career was his father, Sylvain, who was often his coach growing up. Sadly, the day after Pouliot scored his first goal in junior hockey with the Sudbury Wolves, his father died after a battle with leukemia. Pouliot went on to become a top junior and a first pick, fourth overall of the Minnesota Wild in 2005. In 2006-07, he played his first three games with the Wild.

Tom Askey

Mike Kennedy

68

Jaromir Jagr

There has never been any great secret as to why Jaromir Jagr has worn the number 68 throughout his career and exactly what it means to him.

It represents the year—1968—when the Czechoslovakians experienced a brief time of political independence, until the Soviet Union and its allies invaded their country.

It is a reminder of his heritage, he says. But there is also a more personal reason.

"Where to start?" says Jagr. "I grew up on a farm. Our family were like capitalists during the Communist [regime]. My parents had to go to work every day, that's how it was when it was Communist, so I spent a lot of time with my grandmother. She would always talk about the old days, bring up old memories, and she would talk about the Communists and how they took everything from us.

"And all the stories about my grandfather. He died in a jail in 1968. They put him in jail because he had a property and the only way the Communists could take his property was by putting him in jail. So that's why I wear number 68."

Back home, there was never any chance of wearing a number like that, though he has subsequently worn it internationally for the Czech Republic.

"In the Czech Republic we couldn't have a bigger number than 30," he says. "It was the rules. I was number 15 all the time back then."

But he has been number 68 since he came to the NHL for an incredible career that started with the Pittsburgh Penguins, who made him the fifth pick overall in 1990, and continued in Washington and then with the New York Rangers. Jagr won the Stanley Cup twice with the Penguins. He won four straight scoring titles and five overall. He won the Hart Trophy once and was a finalist five times. He won the Pearson Award three times. He captured Olympic gold with the Czech Republic in 1998 and bronze in 2006.

Able to dominate games when he wanted, Jagr has been a prolific scorer and playmaker. He has scored 30 or more goals in 15 straight seasons, missing only in his rookie year, when he had 27. He scored 62 goals and 149 points in 1995-96. He has surpassed 100 points five times. He has held numerous team and league scoring records and has 621 goals and 1,528 points—and counting—in his career.

Many years ago, when he was playing for Pittsburgh alongside Mario Lemieux, it was noted that the letters in his first name could be rearranged to spell "Mario Jr."

And just as Lemieux made 66 famous, hockey fans will always remember 68 for Jagr, who will always have his own special memories.

No. 68

1. **Jaromir Jagr**, Pittsburgh Penguins
2. **Zigmund Palffy**, New York Islanders
3. **Normand Lacombe**, Philadelphia Flyers
4. **Milan Jurcina**, Boston Bruins
5. **Serge Payer**, Florida Panthers
6. **Bruce Hoffort**, Philadelphia Flyers
7. **Eric Nickulas**, St. Louis Blues
8. **Stephen Tepper**, Chicago Blackhawks

Says:

"When he first came up with Pittsburgh, Bob Johnson was the coach, and I remember Bob Johnson telling me that this guy was really going to be something, and he said: 'My biggest problem with him is trying to get him off the ice at practices. I can't get him to come off the ice. The guy just loves hockey.' He hasn't always played as though he loves hockey, especially in Washington. But the other vivid memory I have of Jagr is when he played for Pittsburgh, and this was during one of the times Mario Lemieux wasn't playing, they came to Montreal and played a Sunday afternoon game and he won it all by himself. Pittsburgh was down going into the last period and he came out and he played as good a 20 minutes of hockey as you could ever see a guy play. He's been a very dominant hockey player for the most part of his career and probably, at times, the best player in the world."

Dick Irvin

Zigmund Palffy

Bet You Forgot

New and untested players are often assigned high numbers when starting out in their NHL careers, and so it was for Zigmund Palffy, who was assigned No. 68 his first two seasons with the New York Islanders. But midway through the 1995-96 season and on his way to a team-high 87 points, he switched to No. 16.

Mel Angelstad

Mel Angelstad not only got to live the dream, but he made history in the process.

"I had no idea at the time of the true significance, but guys certainly chuckled about me playing in the NHL and wearing that number," says Angelstad. "I'm thankful now it all happened and I wore the number. Now it's something unique."

No one in the history of the NHL has worn the number 69 in a game except Angelstad. And he wore it for two games in 2004.

"I'm the only one," he says. "I never made any big money from hockey, which is fine, but at least I got some notoriety and I got to play in the NHL and that can't be taken away."

If you are not familiar with the name, it is for good reason. Angelstad, a native of Elstow, Saskatchewan, played 15 seasons of professional hockey everywhere from Thunder Bay (five times) to Nashville to Prince Edward Island (twice) to Phoenix to Fort Worth to Las Vegas to Orlando to Kalamazoo (twice) to Manitoba to Portland (three times) to Belfast (Ireland) to the Motor City (Detroit) to Newcastle (England). By his count he earned close to 5,300 penalty minutes.

But there was one other other stop: Washington. For two games in April 2004.

"The Mangler," as he was known (say MAnglestad and you get it) was famous and a fixture throughout every level of the minors. A hard-nosed winger or defenceman, and a fighter, teams would bring him to town just to sell tickets. He was a modern-day John Brophy.

He didn't even begin playing organized hockey until he was 17, but at 32 the immensely popular Angelstad was signed to an NHL contract by the Capitals (after dozens of fans urged the club to do so) and given his big chance in the NHL, which is when he became the only player ever to wear the number 69. He had two penalty minutes and returned to his life in the minors.

"When I went to Washington for those games, Jaromir Jagr had been traded that year and I said I didn't want his 68, I wanted one better," jokes Angelstad. "But it was my number right from camp. I would have worn any number to be in the NHL."

He had two previous touches with the NHL, attending training camp with Ottawa in 1992 and Dallas in 1999. The latter put him on a line with Mike Modano and Brett Hull and also led to an exhibition game encounter with then-Chicago Blackhawks enforcer Bob Probert and a memorable scrap.

"Probert was the guy I always followed," he says.

Angelstad retired after the 2006 season and completed his studies to become a firefighter in Manitoba.

"If you can believe it, I was voted valedictorian," says Angelstad. "As for the number, every guy on the ice joked that the number suited me perfectly. Hey, my two games I ended up playing 14 minutes a game. I never played that in my life.

"In the first game, against the Rangers, I asked Sandy McCarthy to go, but he said no, the year was over. Same with Chris McAllister. I kept my jersey from that game and got it signed by all the players and coaches and I still have it.

"I always lived by the saying that the only thing that beats talent is hard work and I worked my ass off. But it was worth it, it molded me into a good person."

Says:

"Tough, tough, tough. Fought everybody in every league and racked up the penalty minutes."

Drew Remenda

No. 69

1. **Mel Angelstad**, Washington Capitals

Bet You Forgot

Mel Angelstad gained notoriety for being the only player to wear 69, even if only for two games. But there is another number that was significant to him: 3,700. As in dollars. When he was called up to Washington, the rules stipulated he couldn't return to the minors for the playoffs and Angelstad figures that cost him $3,700 in salary. "I'm probably the only player who lost money playing in the NHL," he says. "But it was worth it."

Mel Angelstad

70

Oleg Tverdovsky

Oleg Tverdovsky's talent has often driven his coaches crazy, only because there has sometimes been a reluctance on the defenceman's part to use it all.

Born in Donetsk in the former Soviet Union, Tverdovsky was Anaheim's first pick, second overall behind Ed Jovanovski in the 1994 Entry Draft, However, in his second season with the Ducks, Tverdovsky was traded to Winnipeg as part of a multi-player deal that brought Teemu Selanne to Anaheim.

Tverdovsky moved with the Jets to Phoenix and played parts of three seasons with the Coyotes before being returned to Anaheim in another trade. He began to show promise in his second go-round with the Ducks, topping 50 points in both the 1999-2000 and 2000-01 seasons and playing with Russia in the 2002 Olympics at Salt Lake City.

That summer, though, he was moved again, this time to New Jersey where he won a Stanley Cup in 2003. Despite that success, Tverdovsky returned to Russia, playing with Avangard Omsk for two seasons before being lured back to the NHL by the Carolina Hurricanes for the 2005-06 season.

With his usual number 10 set aside awaiting retirement in honour of Ron Francis, Tverdovsky switched to number 70 and though he played just five games in the playoffs, won his second Stanley Cup.

Says:

"He has a very high skill level and is willing to take risks from time to time. There's a place for him in the game but I'm probably not the best guy to compliment him because I think that overall he's underachieved for the talent level that he came into the league with."

THOMAS YABLONSKI DELGUIDICE
SAWYER STECKEL

Matt DelGuidice

No. 70

1. **Oleg Tverdovsky**, Carolina Hurricanes
2. **Tim Thomas**, Boston Bruins
3. **Kevin Sawyer**, Phoenix Coyotes
4. **Jeremy Yablonski**, St. Louis Blues
5. **David Steckel**, Washington Capitals
6. **Matt DelGuidice**, Boston Bruins

Tim Thomas

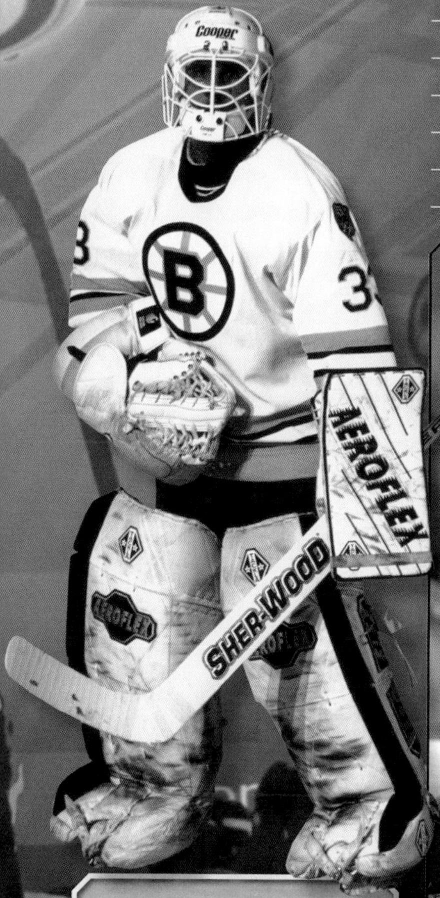

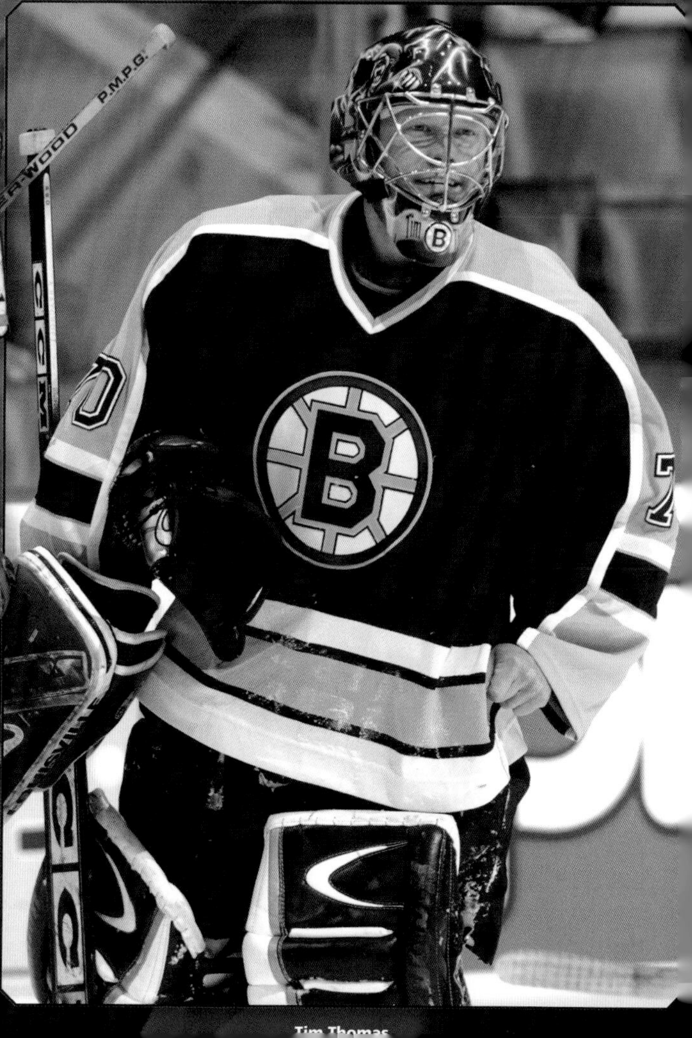

Bet You Forgot

Matt DelGuidice only played 11 NHL games with the Boston Bruins. Had he played against the Buffalo Sabres more often, however, he might have had a longer NHL career. Both of his NHL wins came against the Sabres, 7-4 and 4-2 decisions.

71 Evgeni Malkin

It took longer than Pittsburgh might have wanted, and took a little more work than they would have preferred, but the eventual arrival of Evgeni Malkin in the NHL was worth the wait.

The second pick overall, behind the talented Alexander Ovechkin, in 2004, Malkin appears destined for superstardom with the Penguins. He certainly didn't disappoint in his rookie season, 2006-07. His debut was delayed a year because of transfer and contract issues, then another month once he arrived when he sprained his shoulder in his first exhibition game.

But in his first game with the Penguins he scored against Martin Brodeur, whom he beat again later in the season to score his 30th goal. He ended up finishing with 33 goals and 85 points, his goals, assists, and points all tops amongst rookies. He scored in each of his first six NHL games, a modern-day record.

Malkin at times dazzled with his smooth, powerful skating, his wizardry with the puck, and hard shot.

"He can do things at full speed that some guys would love to be able to do standing still," says Anaheim Ducks general manager Brian Burke. "This kid is going to be a star in this league."

Indeed, Malkin showed prior to joining the Penguins that he could play with men, when he played with the Russian team at the 2006 Olympics and with his club team back home.

In Pittsburgh, the talented forward wore number 71, although 11 was the number he wanted—it was occupied by Jordan Staal.

"When I started to play hockey, I had number 11," Malkin said when he first arrived in Pittsburgh. "It was a prominent number for many, many years (worn internationally by Igor Larionov). When I got to Magnitogorsk, it turned out that the number was given to somebody else. So, I gave it some thought and decided to get a number close to 11 and that's how I came up with 71."

He wore 11 with Russia at the 2007 world hockey championships.

According to Malkin's agent, Pat Brisson, 71 started to become a popular number in Russia because of the 17 worn by former great, the late Valeri Kharlamov.

"I believe they started wearing 71 in his honour," says Brisson. "Because Ilya Kovalchuk (who wears 17 in Atlanta) has international seniority, he wore 71 at the worlds, so Geno had to pick a different number."

Interestingly, according to Penguins beat writer Dave Molinari, Malkin is nicknamed Geno because of his first name, but that is also the nickname that was sometimes given to Jaromir Jagr when he played in Pittsburgh.

CLARK   FOLIGNO   BRISEBOIS
SLEGR   SAVARD

No. 71

1. **Evgeni Malkin**, Pittsburgh Penguins
2. **Wendel Clark**, Detroit Red Wings
3. **Jiri Slegr**, Pittsburgh Penguins
4. **Mike Foligno**, Toronto Maple Leafs
5. **Petr Sykora**, Edmonton Oilers
6. **Marc Savard**, Boston Bruins
7. **Patrice Brisebois**, Colorado Avalanche
8. **Mike Ribeiro**, Montreal Canadiens
9. **Filip Kuba**, Tampa Bay Lightning
10. **Jochen Hecht**, Buffalo Sabres

Jiri Slegr

Mike Foligno

Bet You Forgot

Mike Foligno, who wore 17 with the Buffalo Sabres, reversed it to 71 when he joined the Toronto Maple Leafs because Wendel Clark owned 17. Ironically, when Clark was traded to Detroit from Tampa Bay in the 1998-99 season, he also wore 71 because 17 was being worn by Doug Brown.

Mathieu Schneider

Mathieu Schneider has played for almost as many teams as he's had sweater numbers in the NHL, so he is used to change.

About the only number that really matters to him—the only one with a special significance—is the one he was wearing when he hoisted the Stanley Cup, and even then he has gotten over it years later.

"I had a few numbers in Montreal, but I wore number 27 when we won the Cup there (in 1993)," says Schneider. "I wanted 27 when I went to the New York Islanders, but Derek King had it at the time and he told me I could buy it off him for 50 grand, which was way too much money for me. So I just reversed them for 72."

So how much did he miss 27, because some people care a lot about their numbers—though in his case obviously not $50,000 worth?

"Over the years, it didn't mean a whole lot to me," continues Schneider. "When I was in Montreal, I had three numbers over the six years I was there. I was 18 when I first came in. Then, when they traded for Denis Savard they asked me if he could take 18.

"There weren't a lot of numbers there [because of all the ones that had been retired]. At the time, Montreal really frowned on the high numbers, so I took eight, which I never really liked. That's the one number I had that I was never really crazy about. The first year after I had it, I switched after Shayne Corson got traded and took 27.

"Then, obviously, after winning the Cup there, that became a lucky number for me."

And it got reversed for the next few seasons with the Islanders, then the Leafs. When he got to the New York Rangers, after being dealt by the Leafs, he wore 25, then 21.

"For a change of luck," he says.

Next stop, Los Angeles, where he wore 10, and finally Detroit, where he settled in with 23.

A third-round pick, 44th overall of the Canadiens back in 1987, Schneider has had a good career, playing more than 1,100 games and earning 663 points and the one ring. Once a one-dimensional player, gifted offensively, Schneider developed into a good all-around defenceman, though still very handy on the point on the power play. He signed with Anaheim for the 2007–08 season.

HOCKEY NIGHT

Says:

"The 2005-06 Red Wings boasted Yzerman, Shanahan, and Chelios. Ask any of them to get the real story in the labour war with the NHL & NHLPA, they'd direct you to Schneider. Same with the rules. Tremendous grasp of the game and its issues."

Ron MacLean

No. 72

1. **Mathieu Schneider**, New York Islanders
2. **Ron Hextall**, New York Islanders
3. **Shayne Corson**, Dallas Stars
4. **Brad Smith**, Detroit Red Wings
5. **Peter Schaefer**, Vancouver Canucks
6. **Dave Semenko**, Carolina Hurricanes
7. **Shane Churla**, Los Angeles Kings
8. **Eric Meloche,** Pittsburgh Penguins
9. **Jeff Christian**, Pittsburgh Penguins

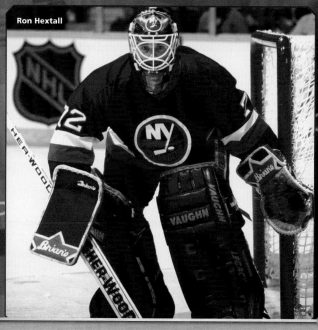

Ron Hextall

Peter Schaefer

Bet You Forgot

Having fiercely protected the net while wearing No. 27 for six seasons in Philadelphia, goaltender Ron Hextall found the number taken by forward Derek King when he signed with the New York Islanders in 1993. Hextall simply reversed the digits and wore No. 72, but reclaimed his old number when he returned to the Flyers the following season.

Michael Ryder

To say scouts had some concerns about Michael Ryder is an understatement.

To say they got it wrong would be dead-on.

Ryder, a native of Bonavista, Newfoundland, was rated 149th by central scouting in 1998, but the Montreal Canadiens didn't select the right winger, who was an offensive force (257 points in three seasons) with Hull and a member of the 2000 world junior team, until the eighth round, 216th overall.

Whatever the reasons, there were doubts that he had what it took to be a good NHL player.

After three years in the minors, Ryder proved everyone wrong.

In 2003-04, Ryder made the Canadiens and as an NHL rookie finished second on the club in scoring with 25 goals and 63 points. He also finished second in voting for the Calder Trophy, even though he tied for the league rookie lead in goals and was first in points.

"In my first training camp, 73 was the number they gave me," says Ryder, who went on to score 30 goals in consecutive seasons. "Every camp after that it was the same number, so when I finally made the team I decided to keep it. In junior I wore 27 for three years and in the minors I wore 26 for three years.

"My first year, with 73, I was thinking, bad number, but I had it again and decided to keep it. To me, the sweater you're wearing is much more important than the number that's on it."

COTE
RYDER   ELICH

No. 73

1. **Michael Ryder**, Montreal Canadiens
2. **Alain Côté**, Quebec Nordiques
3. **Matt Elich**, Tampa Bay Lightning

"To me, there's a little bit of Tomas Holmstrom in him in that he understands what he needs to do to have success. He's got an incredibly hard shot and a quick release that obviously gives goaltenders a real problem, but I think that when he's playing his best he's just a real simple player and he recognizes he doesn't have to do anything fancy to have success."

Kelly Hrudey

Alain Côté

Bet You Forgot

Alain Cote is one of just three players to wear No. 73, donning it fo six games with the Quebec Nordiques in the 1993-94 season. Thoug a journeyman in the NHL, Cote's career has taken him around the globe, suiting up for teams in Japan, Germany, and Finland.

Paul Coffey

There are lots of things by which to remember Paul Coffey as a player—number 74 is not high on the list.

The superstar defenceman wore the number in his final season in the NHL with the Boston Bruins because his two favourite numbers, 7 and 77, were out of circulation, formerly occupied by Phil Esposito and Ray Bourque respectively. Esposito's had been retired, but Coffey wouldn't wear 77 out of respect for Bourque. He apparently wanted something in the 70s and his father suggested 74.

Coffey will always be remembered, though, for his great and graceful skating ability, his blinding speed and ability to weave up ice through defenders, and ultimately his great playmaking and scoring skills. He wasn't bad in his own end, either.

Drafted sixth overall by the Edmonton Oilers in 1980, he was a perfect fit with the young talent Glen Sather assembled. In his first season he had 32 points, but hit his stride the next year when he had 89. The Oilers' number 7 won his first of three career Norris Trophies in 1984-85 when he had a remarkable 121 points in the regular season. That spring, he set playoff records for defencemen with a dozen goals, 25 assists, and 37 points.

His second Norris Trophy arrived the following season when he broke Bobby Orr's goal-scoring record, finishing with 48 and 138 points (just one fewer than Orr had in 1971).

Coffey won the Stanley Cup three times in Edmonton, but contract issues led to him being traded to the Pittsburgh Penguins in 1987. That is when he first switched to number 77. At the time, Rod Buskas was wearing 7 for the Penguins.

Coffey won his fourth and final Stanley Cup in Pittsburgh, then travelled the league, making stops in Los Angeles, Detroit (where he won another Norris), Hartford, Philadelphia, Chicago (just 10 games), Carolina, and Boston for 18 games before retiring in 2000 in his 21st season.

After switching to 77 in Pittsburgh, he wore the number the rest of the way until switching, out of necessity, in Boston.

Coffey finished his incredible career with 396 goals, 1,135 assists, and 1,531 points in the regular season, and with 59 goals and 137 assists in the playoffs. He retired ranked second all-time for defencemen in the regular-season scoring, first for the playoffs.

He was inducted into the Hockey Hall of Fame in 2004 and the Oilers retired his number 7 in 2005.

No. 74

Hockey Night Says:

"Next to Bobby Orr he was the best skater I ever saw. Paul looked like his skates hardly touched the ice. He was always knocked for defensive abilities, but I can still see him [in the 1984 Canada Cup] breaking up that two-on-one rush and taking off with it. He was the second-best offensive defenceman that ever lived."

Don Cherry

1. **Paul Coffey**, Boston Bruins
2. **Jay McKee**, Buffalo Sabres
3. **Brantt Myhres**, Washington Capitals
4. **Steve Larouche**, Ottawa Senators
5. **Nick Tarnasky**, Tampa Bay Lightning

Jay McKee

Steve Larouche

Bet You Forgot

Jay McKee wore 38 when he was first called up to Buffalo, but switched to 74 his first full season (1996-97). He has worn it ever since, although heading into the 2007-08 season with St. Louis he was considering a switch. "It wasn't very lucky for me this year," McKee told reporters, referring to 74 and his first season with the Blues, in which injuries limited him to 23 games. "I'd like to keep the 7. I'll probably go to No. 77."

75

Hal Gill

Hal Gill wasn't exactly a "can't-miss" prospect.

But at 6-foot-7, 250 pounds, he was certainly hard to miss.

Gill was drafted in the eighth round, 207th overall out of Nashoba High School in Bolton, Massachusetts, where he was also a star quarterback who turned down a full football scholarship at Northeastern University.

From there he played four seasons with Providence College, joining the Boston Bruins in 1997.

"When I went to my first camp [in 1997] the number they gave me was 75," says Gill, a native of Concord, Massachusetts. "I wasn't supposed to make the team, but when I did they said, 'What number do you want to wear?' I said 75 is okay, so I just kept it.

"A few months later [in December], they asked me to change numbers because they said it was too close to Ray Bourque's [77]. The people there at the time didn't want high numbers, they were reserved for guys like Bourque, so I had to change, which was fine. I'm not superstitious or crazy about what number I wear, so I switched to 25."

Gill played eight seasons in Boston, including some time alongside Bourque, before signing with the Toronto Maple Leafs as a free agent in July 2006.

A steady, defensive defenceman, Gill still wears 25 in Toronto, where in 2006-07 he had 20 points, two shy of his career best.

Gill has also played for Team USA at four world championships as well as the 2004 World Cup of hockey.

Says:

"Hal Gill is a big body that takes up a big range of the ice surface with his reach, but the thing about Hal that makes him so unique is the fact that he never tries to overdo a play. He lets people come to him, and that's a smart thing to do with a guy that big and with that kind of reach."

Garry Galley

Brett Lindros

No. 75

1. **Hal Gill**, Boston Bruins
2. **Brett Lindros**, New York Islanders
3. **Walt Poddubny**, Quebec Nordiques
4. **Michal Grosek**, Phoenix Coyotes
5. **Colton Orr**, Boston Bruins
6. **Yann Danis**, Montreal Canadiens
7. **Chris Hajt**, Washington Capitals
8. **Desse Roche**, Montreal Canadiens
9. **Leroy Goldsworthy**, Montreal Canadiens
10. **Tony Savage**, Montreal Canadiens

Walt Poddubny

Bet You Forgot

Walt Poddubny wore No. 75 during his one season with the Quebec Nordiques in 1988-89. A decent offensive player with the Maple Leafs in the early 80s, Poddubny blossomed when he joine

76

Dustin Penner

With his name freshly inscribed on the Stanley Cup, Anaheim's Dustin Penner is likely resisting the urge to tell many NHL scouts, "I told you so."

Undrafted, the Winkler, Manitoba, native was playing on a scholarship at the University of Maine when the Ducks offered him a contract in 2004. Penner then spent two seasons in the minors before cracking the Anaheim lineup in 2005-06, playing 19 games and registering seven points.

With his size—6-foot-4, 245 pounds—his most obvious asset, Penner impressed new general manager Brian Burke in the 2006-07 season and he was given a regular spot in the lineup, playing all 82 games and scoring 29 goals and 45 points. As well as a roster spot, Burke gave Penner a new number because he didn't like high numbers such as Penners' No. 76.

"I picked 17, but for no particular reason," said Penner, whose teammates Ryan Getzlaf and Corey Perry were also told to switch to lower numbers.

Whether it had an effect or not, all three were major contributors in the 2007 playoffs as the Ducks became the first team from California to win a Stanley Cup, defeating the Ottawa Senators in five games.

Penner, who was a restricted free agent, signed with the Edmonton Oilers in the summer of 2007.

"He's going to be a great hockey player. Obviously being thrown into the Stanley Cup early in his career like this and showing the poise, class, and toughness he demonstrated shows you that he's got a great future."

Radek Bonk

No. 76

1. **Dustin Penner**, Anaheim Ducks
2. **Radek Bonk**, Ottawa Senators
3. **Wayne Primeau**, Buffalo Sabres
4. **Richard Park**, Pittsburgh Penguins
5. **Andrew Peters**, Buffalo Sabres
6. **Dennis Bonvie**, Boston Bruins
7. **Darcy Verot,** Washington Capitals
8. **Kris Vernarsky**, Boston Bruins
9. **Jozef Balej**, Montreal Canadiens
10. **Evgeny Artyukhin**, Tampa Bay Lightning

Bet You Forgot

Czech-born Radek Bonk was touted as an offensive star when, as a 17-year-old, he played professionally for the Las Vegas Thunder of the International Hockey League. Drafted third overall by Ottawa in the 1994 entry draft, the desperate Senators waited for his scoring prowess to kick in. While he had some respectable seasons wearing No. 76 for the Senators, his true value emerged as a defensive forward.

77

Ray Bourque

Raymond Bourque is a player who could easily be remembered for making two numbers famous and, in his case, he also will always be remembered for how he made the transition from one number to the next.

When he arrived in Boston in 1979, after being selected eighth overall by the Boston Bruins, Bourque was good right away. He won the Calder Trophy and was an all-star. And as quickly as he was good, he was great.

In his first training camp with the Bruins, he was given the number 29, which he wore during the exhibition games. Once the regular season started, he was given number seven, a significant number in Boston because the previous owner was Phil Esposito, who had been traded to the New York Rangers four years earlier.

Bourque was a force on the Bruins' blue line, as good defensively as he was offensively. A perennial all-star, he won the Norris Trophy five times, the Lester Patrick, and lost out on the Hart by the narrowest of margins in 1990. He was captain for 14 seasons, the longest run in team history. He is the all-time NHL leader for defencemen in points (1,579), goals (410), and assists (1,169). His list of achievements is long.

Always regarded as being a classy player, that point was driven home in December 1987, when the Bruins honoured Esposito and number 7. The plan was once Bourque retired, the number would be retired, too. But that night, during the ceremony, Bourque slipped off his usual number 7 and handed it to Esposito. Underneath, Bourque was wearing a second Bruins sweater with number 77 on the back.

About the only regret Bourque had in his remarkable 21 seasons in Boston is that despite a couple of trips to the finals, he wasn't able to win the Stanley Cup with the Bruins. That only happened after he was traded to the Colorado Avalanche. In his 22nd season, number 77 finally won the big prize, allowing him to retire fulfilled. His was the longest wait of any NHL player.

Bourque's number 77 was retired by both the Bruins and the Avalanche, despite his short stay, and he was inducted into the Hockey Hall of Fame in 2004.

No. 77

1. **Ray Bourque**, Boston Bruins
2. **Paul Coffey**, Pittsburgh Penguins
3. **Phil Esposito**, New York Rangers
4. **Adam Oates**, Anaheim Ducks
5. **Pierre Turgeon**, Buffalo Sabres
6. **Garry Unger**, Los Angeles Kings
7. **Cliff Ronning**, New York Islanders
8. **Alexei Zhitnik**, New York Islanders
9. **Chris Gratton**, Tampa Bay Lightning
10. **Anson Carter**, Columbus Blue Jackets

Hockey Night in Canada Says:

"The best captain I ever played for and a great friend. I certainly learned tons just sitting on the bench watching him go out there and play 40 minutes a game. Ray gave up the opportunity to really stack up a ton of points and get into that Coffey and Leetch set, guys that were scoring tons of points; he gave that up to play at both ends of the ice surface. I think that's what really got him the respect of a lot of his peers. He had 70 points but he played like a bear in his end."

Garry Galley

Adam Oates

Phil Esposito

Bet You Forgot

This is a popular number for players who also wore No. 7. Those

Pavol Demitra

Sentiment and superstition don't always attach themselves to players' numbers, so when he was assigned number 78 by the Ottawa Senators at his first training camp in 1993, Pavol Demitra simply kept it.

Drafted in the ninth round of the 1993 Entry Draft, Demitra spent parts of three seasons with the Senators but couldn't crack the woeful Ottawa lineup on a regular basis and in November 1996 he was traded to the St. Louis Blues and switched to number 38.

There the Czech native's game blossomed, playing in the All-Star game in 1999, 2000, and 2002 as well as winning the Lady Byng Trophy in 2000, when he registered 75 points with just eight penalty minutes.

He would play seven full seasons in St. Louis, his best being 2002-03 when he scored 36 goals and 93 points. After spending the lockout season playing in Slovakia, he signed as a free agent with the Los Angeles Kings before the 2005-06 season and though he had 62 points, was traded at the 2006 Entry Draft to the Minnesota Wild, where he was hooked up with young star Marian Gaborik.

LANDRY
POULIOT

Says:

"I think he's one of the guys that's come over that's a pure points guy. He just has the ability to see the ice well, good skater; unfortunately, injuries have kept him from reaching his full potential. He's one of those guys you always have to be aware of when you're on the ice."

Garry Galley

No. 78

1. **Pavol Demitra**, Ottawa Senators
2. **Eric Landry**, Montreal Canadiens
3. **Marc-Antoine Pouliot**, Edmonton Oilers

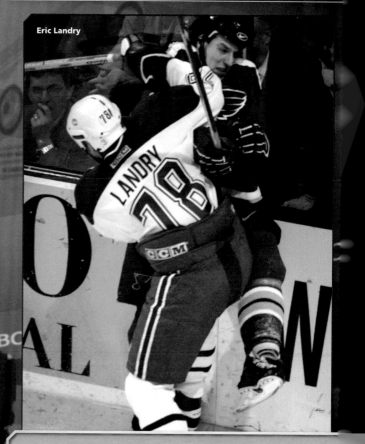

Eric Landry

Bet You Forgot

Another player to wear 78 was Eric Landry, a hard-nosed player who was originally signed by Calgary as a free agent in 1997. He was later traded to San Jose, where he never played in the NHL. The Gatineau native was then signed by Montreal as a free agent in 2000. He wore 11 and 26 with the Flames and was assigned 78 by the Habs. He played a total of 68 NHL games, earning 14 points, 11 of them coming in that first season with the Habs.

79

Alexei Yashin

To say that Alexei Yashin's career has been controversial and eventful is an understatement.

To say he peaked early would simply be accurate.

Yashin was the first-ever player drafted by the Ottawa Senators, second overall in 1992. He didn't play with the expansion team until a year later, but when he did he made a big impact, earning 79 points in his rookie season. He continued to improve and put together back-to-back 30-goal seasons, then had a 44-goal, 94-point breakthrough in 1998-99, the same year he became the first Russian captain of an NHL team and was runner-up for the Hart Trophy.

The slick centre had already had a dandy contract battle in Ottawa, but after that big season another ensued, with Yashin ultimately sitting out the year, demanding a trade. He eventually played a year later after he was ordered to return by an arbitrator—and he played well, getting 88 points—but that finally led to the draft-day deal in 2001 to the Islanders for defenceman Zdeno Chara, winger Bill Muckalt, and a draft pick that turned out to be Jason Spezza.

Yashin had worn 19 with the Senators, but he couldn't wear that number when he joined the Islanders because it had been retired for Bryan Trottier. So he chose 79—in part, he said, because it looks like 19, and in part because that's how many points he'd scored in his rookie season.

A high number, it wasn't as high as the number on the contract he was given by the Islanders: an incredible 10-year, $87.5 million package. But after earning 75 points his first season in New York, he could never recapture that form and, finally, after being benched at home in the 2007 playoffs, the Islanders' captain was bought out of the remaining four years of his deal, worth a little more than $17 million.

"I wish someone could sit him down and talk to him and harness all that great talent. There's no question about it: the talent is there, but it's been bottled up too long and he won't let go. He'll have great nights for you but that's no good in this league. It has to be more frequent and unfortunately

MARKOV
VUJTEK

Andrei Markov

No. 79

1. **Alexei Yashin**, New York Islanders
2. **Andrei Markov**, Montreal Canadiens
3. **Vladimir Vujtek**, Tampa Bay Lightning

Vladimir Vujtek

Bet You Forgot

Andrei Markov, drafted 162nd overall in 1998, debuted with the Canadiens in 2000 wearing No. 79. "That was the number given to me," he says. In the summer of 2007, he signed a four-year, $23-million contract with Montreal. Not many players wear 79, but most have been well paid. Back home in Russia he wore 25 and has worn 52 internationally when 79 or 25 have not been available.

Nik Antropov

Nik Antropov made history when he became the first player from Kazakhstan to be taken in the NHL draft.

The year was 1998 and the Toronto Maple Leafs selected the 6-foot-6 centre 10th overall. However, the combination of youth and injuries, including multiple knee operations, slowed his development.

But in 2006-07, the Leafs saw vast improvement from the young forward, who mostly played alongside captain Mats Sundin. Antropov improved his skating and his physical play and appeared his most confident.

When he arrived in Toronto as a 19-year-old with limited English, he first wore number 9. "That is the number they gave me," says Antropov, whose best season statistically was 2002-03, when he played 72 games and had 45 points. Even in 2006-07 he fought through injuries, managing 33 points in 54 games. "I was going to choose 19, but Fred Modin was wearing it. My other favourite number was 11 and Steve Sullivan had it. I was going to go to a higher number, but they said wear 9."

After Sullivan departed, Antropov was able to switch.

"I switched to 11 after two seasons, but gave it up when Owen Nolan came to our team," he says. "I asked him if he would like it and he said you don't have to, but if you're being a nice guy I will take it. I couldn't take 19 because Mikael Renberg had it. So I took 80, the year I was born."

Although motivated by generosity, Antropov no doubt was hoping for a change in luck, which hasn't entirely happened. But he has seen his game improve wearing number 80.

Says:

"He's serviceable at being a utility guy. He can play left wing, right wing, and centre, although I think naturally, he's a better centre than anywhere else. He's got great size. He's a typical Russian in that he'd love to beat you one-on-one and he's got great poise with the puck and patience when he has the puck. As far as being a serviceable two-way forward he fills that need. I think there are too many times where he takes shifts off where he could be dominant because he has such puck skills. He should score way more than he does."

Drew Remenda

No. 80

1. **Nik Antropov**, Toronto Maple Leafs
2. **Geoff Sanderson**, Buffalo Sabres
3. **Kevin Weekes**, New York Islanders
4. **Steve McLaren**, St. Louis Blues

Geoff Sanderson

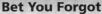

Kevin Weekes

Bet You Forgot

Geoff Sanderson wore 8 for a number of good years with the Hartford Whalers, but when he eventually made his way to Buffalo that number was taken by defenceman Darryl Shannon, so he made the practical switch to 80. Whenever he had the chance, in Columbus and Phoenix and Philadelphia, he always switched back to 8. When he first arrived in Hartford as a rookie he wore 13.

Miroslav Satan

Every once in a while teams strike gold, planned or not, when making trades. And so it was with the Buffalo Sabres when they picked up Miroslav Satan.

Shortly after arriving in a deal with the Edmonton Oilers for the unheralded Craig Millar and Barrie Moore, the talented winger found his stride and led the Sabres in scoring for several seasons, including scoring 40 goals in 1998-99.

Satan, whose name is pronounced Sha-tuhn, was drafted 111th overall in 1993 by Edmonton, where he played for parts of two seasons. The Slovak had eight good years with the Sabres, scoring 20 or more goals in seven straight seasons, before moving to the New York Islanders in 2005 as a free agent. With the Isles he had 35- and 27-goal seasons.

When he was with the Oilers, Satan wore number 32 for most of his 126 games. When he got to Buffalo he wanted his favoured number 18, but it was taken by Michal Grosek.

"I used to be number 18 and when I came to Buffalo it was taken, so I chose 81 because it is 18 reversed," says Satan.

When Grosek left, he tried 18 briefly, but slumped and wound up changing back to 81.

"It seemed like nobody liked 18, so I switched it back to 81," he said at the time. "Nobody liked it, that I was struggling. Everybody made me feel bad about it. So I had to switch back to 81."

The number was eventually retired to honour Danny Gare, a long-time Sabres star and former captain.

Says:

"Just a goal scorer. This guy has a knack around the net. He's not a guy that's going to be overly physical, he's a really wiry kind of guy that finds holes through the ice surface and doesn't seem to get hit very much, but around the net he's very dangerous."

Garry Galley

No. 81

1. **Miroslav Satan**, Buffalo Sabres
2. **Marcel Hossa,** New York Rangers
3. **Mike Sillinger**, Nashville Predators
4. **Phil Kessel**, Boston Bruins
5. **Fedor Fedorov**, Vancouver Canucks
6. **Craig Laughlin**, Los Angeles Kings

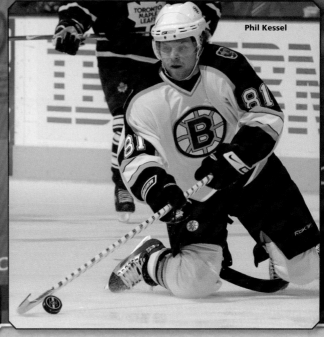

Phil Kessel

Craig Laughlin

Bet You Forgot

Boston Bruins centre Phil Kessel had an unforgettable rookie season for reasons both good and bad. The fifth overall pick in 2006, Kessel had 29 points in 70 games. But in December, the 19-year-old had to undergo surgery for testicular cancer. He returned 11 games later and won the Masterton Trophy for his perseverance. At the University of Minnesota he wore No. 26, but opted for 81 with Boston because his favoured 8 was retired in honour of Cam Neely and 81 was his first number at the US National Team Development Program.

82

Martin Straka

At various times in his 14-year career, Martin Straka has proven he can be a front-line NHL player. He just hasn't done it consistently, although he has strung together good seasons, back-to-back, with the New York Rangers.

Straka was a first-round pick, 19th overall, by the Pittsburgh Penguins back in 1992. After a couple of seasons with the Penguins, he was traded to the Ottawa Senators, who less than a year later moved him to the New York Islanders as part of a package that netted them, in part, defenceman Wade Redden, who has become a mainstay on the Ottawa blue line.

The same spring Straka landed in Long Island, he was placed on waivers and claimed by the Florida Panthers. Straka eventually found his way back as a free agent to Pittsburgh, where he spent seven seasons, before being moved to Los Angeles in 2003 as part of a cash dump. He signed with the Rangers as a free agent in the summer of 2005 and has played some of his best hockey in New York, earning another contract.

Injuries have had a big impact on Straka's career and have affected his consistency. His best season was 2000-01 when he had 95 points. The past two seasons in New York he has had 76 and 70 respectively.

On the international scene, Straka won gold with the Czech Republic in the 1998 Winter Olympics and in the 2005 world hockey championships.

As for his choice of sweater number 82, a limited number of options forced him to be creative.

"I wore 28 back home in the Czech Republic 14 years ago and when I got to Pittsburgh all the jerseys, 22, 24, 26, 28 were taken," explains Straka. "So I just switched to 82. No other reason really."

Says:

"The years in Pittsburgh when everything was kind of drying out and the big guns were all leaving he was a guy that kept stepping up there and really did a hell of a job. Everywhere he goes he seems to find a way to make it work, and not every player can do that."

Marian Gaborik

No. 82

1. **Martin Straka**, Pittsburgh Penguins
2. **Marian Gaborik**, Minnesota Wild
3. **Donald Audette**, Montreal Canadiens

Donald Audette

Bet You Forgot

Born in 1982, Marian Gaborik experimented with wearing the No. 82 in his rookie season of 2000-01 with the expansion Minnesota Wild. He wore it for only a few games, however, before switching back to his usual No. 10. The Wild's first draft pick, third overall in 2000, Gaborik scored the team's first goal in the franchise's first game on October 6, 2000. At 18 years of age, he was also the youngest player to score a team's first goal.

Ales Hemsky

Ales Hemsky was a first-round pick of the Edmonton Oilers, 13th overall, in the 2001 Entry Draft.

Born in Pardubice, Czech Republic on August 13, 1983, Hemsky has worn number 83 since breaking in with the Oilers in 2002-03.

The left winger played 59 games that first season, scoring six goals and 30 points. His best year so far was 2005-06 when he had 77 points in 81 games, including 58 assists. He also had 17 points in the playoffs as the Oilers went to Game 7 of the Stanley Cup final before losing to Carolina.

He also played for the Czech Republic at the 2006 Olympics, skating on a line with Jaromir Jagr and winning a bronze medal.

Says:

"Without question he's in the top five percent in the National Hockey League in skill level, but I just don't think he's ever had to work at understanding the game because his skill level growing up was just higher than everybody else. So he is like (Alexei) Kovalev and a couple of others in that he just doesn't really understand how to get the most out of himself and his teammates and until he does he's going to be a highly skilled player that underachieves. But he has the potential to be an absolute superstar in the game."

Kelly Hrudey

No. 83

1. **Ales Hemsky**, Edmonton Oilers
2. **Domenic Pittis**, Buffalo Sabres
3. **Eric Bertrand**, Montreal Canadiens
4. **Matt Foy**, Minnesota Wild
5. **Pat Leahy**, Boston Bruins

Eric Bertrand

Domenic Pittis

Bet You Forgot

This is neither a popular nor accomplished number in the NHL, with Buffalo's Domenic Pittis having played the second-most games (86) of the five players who have worn it.

84 Guillaume Latendresse

The first time Guillaume Latendresse stepped on the ice wearing his Montreal Canadiens sweater he made history and didn't even know it.

A second-round pick of the Canadiens in 2005 out of Drummondville, Latendresse wasn't expected to make the club in 2006–07, but the 19-year-old impressed both coach Guy Carbonneau and general manager Bob Gainey, who felt he would develop more at the NHL level and signed him to a contract. And when he appeared wearing sweater number 84 he became the first NHL player to ever wear that number in a game. It was the last number, from 0 to 99, to be filled.

"There is no significance to it whatsover," shrugged Latendresse. "It's the number they gave me at training camp. I liked it and decided to keep it. I was just happy to be wearing a Canadiens sweater, it didn't matter what was on the back. What mattered is what was on the front.

"In junior I wore 22. But a number is just a number, it doesn't matter. The sweater matters."

Latendresse, a member of the gold-medal-winning 2005 Canadian world junior team, but who seldom played, has quickly become a favourite of Canadiens fans.

Interestingly, Latendresse unwittingly was drawn into a controversy with legendary goaltender Patrick Roy last season. After it took the youngster 14 games to score his first goal, Roy questioned why the right winger wasn't returned to junior and suggested it was only because he was Francophone.

"As soon as I hear his name in a question, I say 'next question,'" Latendresse told reporters. "It's me who's supposed to be 19, not him. I will act like a man. I'll leave it to him to act like a child. I don't know why he's acting like that. I've never spoken to him. He should be delighted by the success of young Quebecers in the NHL instead of making stupid comments."

Latendresse wound up playing in 80 games during his rookie season, scoring 16 goals and adding 13 assists.

No. 84

1. **Guillaume Latendresse**, Montreal Canadiens

Says:

"I'll say this for him, that kid came up with tremendous pressure put on him by the media in Montreal and he responded pretty well. He seemed to handle it in his interviews and everything and I thought that he showed a maturity for a player his age and stage in his first year in the NHL. And he had a lot more pressure than most rookies have because of the reaction of the media. He handled it very well and I give him credit for that."

Dick Irvin

Guillaume Latendresse

Petr Klima

It was in the late summer of 1985 that Petr Klima, who had long been coveted by the Detroit Red Wings, finally defected from his native Czechoslovakia.

That is why he wore the number 85, as a reminder.

Although a handful of players had defected to Canadian-based NHL teams previously, Klima was the first to go to an American team. Not a big player, Klima had great speed and skill, a natural scorer. But, whether it was the change of lifestyle, language issues, or just his personality, he was also a bit erratic on and off the ice, and very much an enigma to his coaches.

Drafted 86th overall in 1983, Klima had made it known to the Red Wings that until he fulfilled his military obligations he would not seek his freedom. Once the former was done, the Red Wings went to work.

Klima, who had some off-ice issues, wound up playing a little more than four seasons in Detroit before being dealt, along with Joe Murphy and Adam Graves, to the Edmonton Oilers, where he helped win a Stanley Cup in 1990. In Edmonton, he had a 40-goal season and scored a triple-overtime goal against Boston in the final.

But inconsistent play had him on the move again, this time to Tampa Bay, then quick stops in Los Angeles and Pittsburgh, before making cameo appearances again in Edmonton, where he was let go. He had one last kick at it in Detroit, but that is where his colourful NHL journey started and ultimately ended in 1999.

The personable left winger finished his career with 313 goals and 573 points in 786 games.

Says:

"He was a happy-go-lucky guy, great around the team, and he sat on the bench (for Edmonton in the Cup final against Boston) and didn't make any noises, and didn't get into the game in Boston very much in that long, long playoff game in the Boston Garden. But he was thrown out there and it was a big move and he got the big goal. But that was the type Petr was. He was given a job to do and he did it."

Bob Cole

No. 85

1. **Petr Klima**, Detroit Red Wings
2. **Rostislav Olesz**, Florida Panthers

Rostislav Olesz

Bet You Forgot

Only two players have ever worn No. 85 and both just happened to be natives of the Czech Republic. The most recent is Rostislav Olesz of the Florida Panthers, who was born in 1985.

86

Jonathan Ferland

Like a lot of young players, Jonathan Ferland simply took the number he was given and was just happy to be wearing the sweater.

Now, of course, he can't wait to get it back.

Ferland, a right winger out of Quebec City drafted 212th overall by the Canadiens in 2002, was called up for seven games by Montreal during the 2005-06 season from the American Hockey League Hamilton Bulldogs. In his NHL debut, on January 3, 2006, wearing number 86, the only player in the NHL to ever wear the number, Ferland scored on Pittsburgh Penguins goaltender Marc-Andre Fleury, in a 6-4 loss.

Ferland managed just the one goal, nine shots, and two penalty minutes in his seven games (he was also minus-two) before he was returned to Hamilton, where he has remained and where he wears number 21 with the Bulldogs.

"I've worn 21, 22, or 24 all my career, but that's what they gave me when I [first] went to Montreal," Ferland said. "Usually, in Montreal they give you a high number and then when you make the team they ask you about a number.

"If I go back there, go up, I think I'm stuck with that. I wouldn't change it now, anyway. I played my first seven games with that number and I would keep it now. Another team, I might want something different but I'll be sticking with that one in Montreal. It looks good to me. I think it brought me luck because I scored in my first game."

No. 86

1. **Jonathan Ferland**, Montreal Canadiens

Jonathan Ferland

Sidney Crosby

Sidney Crosby wasn't the first player to wear the number 87.

But he will quite likely be the last.

And just like Wayne Gretzky with the number 99, and Mario Lemieux with 66, Crosby and 87 have become synonymous.

"August 7, 1987," says Crosby, explaining the significance of the number. "Eighth month, seventh day, 87th year."

And just like Gretzky and Lemieux, Sid the Kid is destined to attain a special status in the game, or perhaps we should say an even more special status because his greatness has been on full display through his first two NHL seasons.

Indeed, even his arrival in the NHL was unique. After the league shut down business for a season, they used a special weighted lottery to determine the draft order in the summer of 2005. The big winners were the Pittsburgh Penguins, who were actually for sale before the lottery but not after they were given the number one pick.

In many ways, Crosby saved a franchise that was in desperate need of improvement and a new arena. There was no way the civic fathers were letting the Penguins and Crosby leave Pittsburgh.

A phenom as a kid growing up in Cole Harbour, Nova Scotia, then as a junior in Rimouski, some wondered if Crosby would have the same impact as a pro. In his rookie season, Crosby did not disappoint. He finished sixth in the league in scoring with 39 goals and 102 points and was a human highlight reel. In his second season, Crosby won the scoring title with 36 goals and 120 points, leading the Penguins to the playoffs for the first time in five seasons in the process.

At 19, he became the youngest player to reach 200 points—at 19 years, 207 days—and the youngest player to win the Art Ross Trophy.

When the Penguins named him captain on May 31, 2007, Crosby also became the youngest full-time captain in NHL history at 19 years, 297 days.

Growing up, Crosby attained notoriety and made headlines at an early age. As a junior, he was endorsed by none other than Gretzky as being the real thing. As a kid, Steve Yzerman was one of his idols and he looked up to both the Red Wings star and Peter Forsberg. In midget hockey in Dartmouth and with the Canadian junior team, which didn't allow the number 87 to be worn, he wore number 9, in part because his family were all Montreal Canadiens fans.

"I wore nine as a kid, Rocket (Richard) was big in the province," says Crosby. "But in junior it was 87. It was the first time for big numbers."

The first time, that is, for big numbers that aren't in the scoring statistics.

No. 87

1. **Sidney Crosby**, Pittsburgh Penguins
2. **Pierre Turgeon**, Colorado Avalanche
3. **Donald Brashear**, Philadelphia Flyers

HOCKEY NIGHT Says:

"He's the face of the NHL at the age of 19. I mean, who else does commercials on television? This kid has had two years and maybe, with the exception of Wayne Gretzky, maybe at the end of two years he's made as big an impression as anybody has ever made at that age. So maybe he is the next one, as we used to say."

Dick Irvin

Donald Brashear

Pierre Turgeon

Bet You Forgot

Pierre Turgeon's number choice with the Colorado Avalanche was an apt reminder of his draft year when the Buffalo Sabres selected him first overall in 1987. His selection proved worthwhile as he has scored more than 500 goals and 1,300 points since then.

88 Eric Lindros

Though tagged with the moniker "The Next One," Eric Lindros' double-digit number in no way was meant to mimic the players he was supposed to supplant—Wayne Gretzky and his 99 or Mario Lemieux and 66.

Rather, Eric Lindros chose 88 as a tribute to the late John McCauley, who wore number 8 as an NHL referee. The father of a teammate on his junior team, the Junior B St. Michael's Majors, McCauley gave Lindros advice and wisdom as the 15-year-old star endured criticism and cheap shots from the older players in the league. When Lindros went to the Oshawa Generals of the Ontario Hockey League, the number 8 he had worn with St. Mike's was taken by captain Iain Frasier so he switched to 88 and wore it throughout his career.

Unfortunately for Lindros, it has been a career that has fallen short of those early accolades, mostly because of a series of head injuries that have kept him out for extended periods.

Taken number one by the Quebec Nordiques in the 1991 Entry Draft, Lindros refused to sign with the team and was ultimately traded to Philadelphia. Things began well there, and in 1994-95 he tied for the league lead in points (70 in a shortened season) and won the Hart Trophy as MVP. In 1998 he was named captain of Team Canada at the Nagano Olympics, a team that included many stars, including Gretzky, but failed to win a medal. Lindros had won a silver with Canada at the 1992 Olympics.

In 1999, injuries began to take their toll and a collapsed lung kept him out of the lineup in a playoff loss to the Leafs. The following season he suffered four concussions, the worst from a hit by New Jersey's Scott Stevens in the semifinals.

With his relationship with Flyers general manager Bobby Clarke in tatters, Lindros wound up missing the 2000-01 season as Clarke refused to accommodate his wishes for a trade, and disagreements over his medical care spilled into the newspapers. In the fall of 2001, however, Lindros was dealt to the New York Rangers. He played decently, scoring 36 goals and 73 points in 2001-02, but the controlled fury that had marked his earlier stardom was no longer evident. Injuries continued to plague him in New York and in Toronto two years later. He played the 2006-07 season with the Dallas Stars.

Says:

"He was a terrific power forward, just like Neely. He had greatness painted all over him, it's just unfortunate he had all those concussions. He's a great kid. I still remember when he was 18, in the Canada Cup, he broke Ulf Samuelsson's shoulder—how could I think bad of him? He had all the potential and still had a great career, but not the one we all thought."

Don Cherry

Joe Sakic

No. 88

1. **Eric Lindros**, Philadelphia Flyers
2. **Joe Sakic**, Quebec Nordiques
3. **Ken Hodge**, New York Rangers
4. **Owen Nolan**, Quebec Nordiques
5. **Christopher Higgins**, Montreal Canadiens
6. **Garry Howatt**, New Jersey Devils
7. **Rocky Trottier**, New Jersey Devils
8. **Xavier Delisle**, Montreal Canadiens
9. **Roger Jenkins**, Montreal Canadiens

Owen Nolan

Bet You Forgot

Although both Joe Sakic and Owen Nolan both wore number 88 in their respective rookie years with the Quebec Nordiques, Eric Lindros had nothing to do with it. Both wore the number before Lindros was drafted, and both immediately switched to their preferred numbers as soon as they became available. No Nordique wore 88 after Lindros was drafted in 1991.

Alex Mogilny

When Alexander Mogilny arrived in Buffalo, the Sabres had the number 89 hanging in his stall waiting for him.

The reason?

It was in 1989 that the talented winger left Russia to play in the NHL and Mogilny was the 89th pick overall in the previous year's draft. So the number just felt right. He was asked if he was okay with it and the answer was yes.

In Russia, Mogilny had played with CSKA Moscow, where he wore number 14, and the gold-medal Olympic team in 1988. He had played on a terrific line with Sergei Fedorov and Pavel Bure, all three achieving great success on their own in the NHL. It was after the 1989 world championships, though, that Mogilny defected to North America.

Mogilny pretty much lived up to his advance billing, too, becoming known as Alexander the Great to Sabres fans for his electrifying play, especially in his fourth season when he scored 76 goals and 127 points, his best year ever in the league. He tied Teemu Selanne in goals, but became the first Russian to lead the league.

While always a terrific player and a dangerous scorer, Mogilny only once came close to those numbers again, always being very good but not always great, as his career drifted through stops in Vancouver, New Jersey, where he won the Stanley Cup, Toronto, and finally New Jersey again, where ongoing hip problems forced him to the sidelines all of 2006-07.

He had eight seasons with 30 or more goals, scored 473 career goals and 1,032 points and won the Lady Byng Trophy in 2003.

Mogilny is also one of just 19 players in the world to belong to what is called the Triple Gold Club—winners of the Stanley Cup, as well as gold in the Olympics and world championships.

"Never mind opposing goaltenders, he terrified journalists."

Ron MacLean

COMRIE TURCOTTE CHYZOWSKI

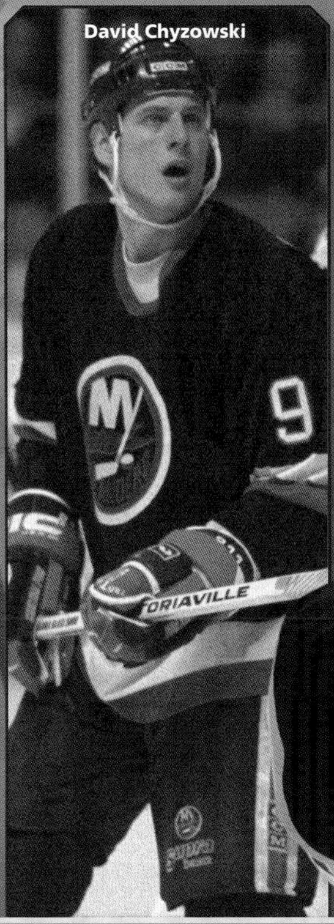

David Chyzowski

No. 89

1. **Alexander Mogilny**, Buffalo Sabres
2. **Mike Comrie**, Edmonton Oilers
3. **Darren Turcotte**, Winnipeg Jets
4. **David Chyzowski**, New York Islanders
5. **Zdenek Blatny**, Boston Bruins

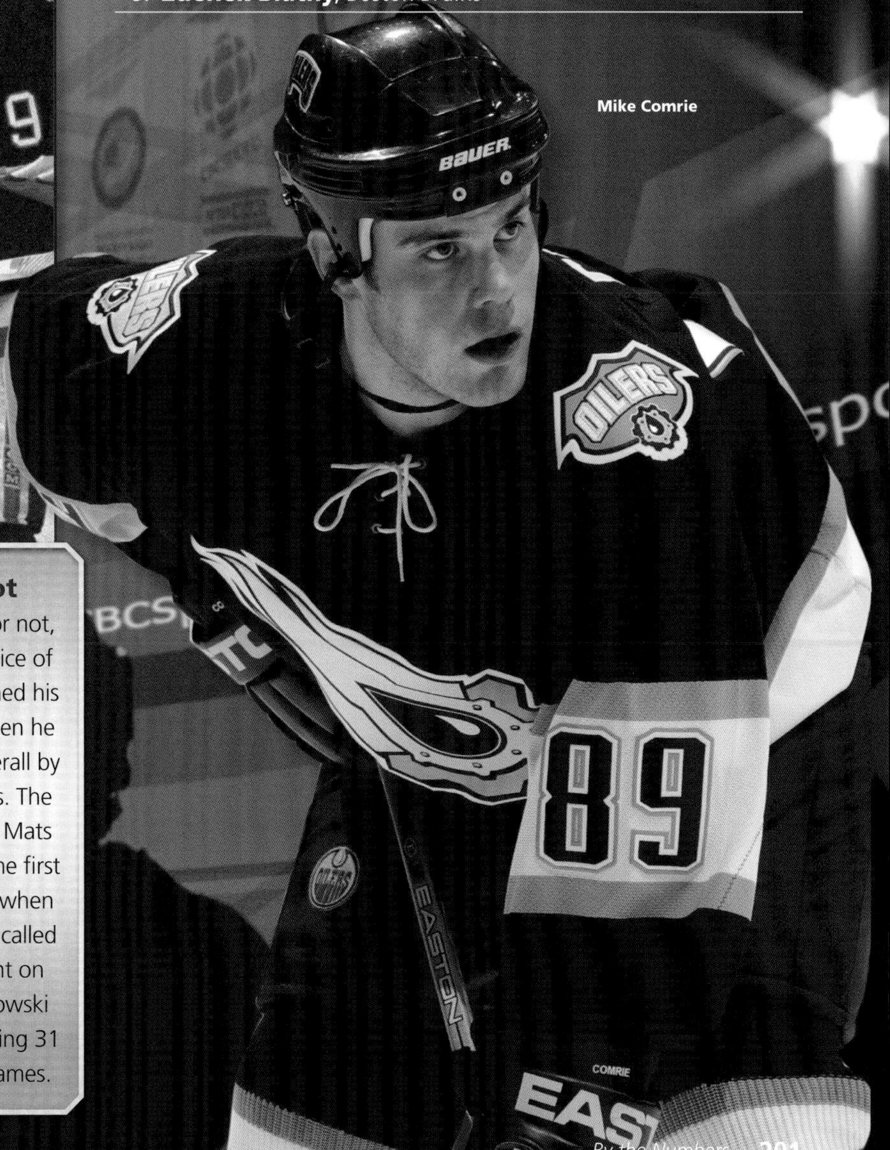

Mike Comrie

Bet You Forgot

Either by coincidence or not, David Chyzowski's choice of uniform number matched his draft year—1989—when he was chosen second overall by the New York Islanders. The top pick that year was Mats Sundin, who became the first European taken No. 1 when the Quebec Nordiques called his name. Sundin went on to be a star, but Chyzowski never panned out, scoring 31 points in 126 career games.

Joe Juneau

Hockey isn't rocket science, but it doesn't mean you can't be a rocket scientist to play the game.

And Joe Juneau is a rocket scientist of sorts. He earned a degree in aeronautical engineering in just three years at Rensselaer Polytechnic Institute, while also playing hockey, earning two All-American selections in the process. Did we mention he didn't speak English when he first arrived at the school? Yes, he is a bright guy.

Juneau was drafted by the Boston Bruins in the fourth round in 1988 and wound up playing for Washington, Buffalo, Ottawa, Phoenix, and Montreal before retiring in 2004. He was generally regarded as a good, solid two-way player.

His post-college career actually started with the Canadian Olympic team after a contract dispute with the Bruins. He helped Canada win silver at the Albertville Games, and then joined the Bruins late in 1992.

Prior to the Olympic experience, Juneau had threatened to play in Switzerland, to which Bruins general manager Harry Sinden said, "Then he better learn to yodel."

In his rookie year, playing alongside Cam Neely and Adam Oates, he had 32 goals and 102 points, setting the league record for assists by a rookie left winger with 70. He was runner-up in Calder Trophy voting.

He was later traded to Washington, where he helped the Capitals reach the Stanley Cup finals. After that, he made the rounds in the NHL before finally retiring and has spent considerable time teaching kids in Nunavut to play hockey.

Juneau had always worn number 9 as a kid, but when he arrived in Boston it was retired in honour of Johnny Bucyk. There was a story going around that Juneau asked if he could wear that number, but he says, "That would have been disrespectful, I wouldn't do that.

"I asked if I could wear 90, but Harry Sinden said no, no one has a number higher than Ray Bourque (77). Then I thought, okay, 49. Number 4 for Bobby Orr and 9 for Bucyk and 9 was my favourite number."

As Juneau later found out, 49 had another attachment: Alaska is the 49th state and Juneau happens to be the capital city.

"I found that out later, it was pretty funny, but it made it an even better fit," he says.

Anyway, throughout his career he tried to have a 9 in his number and wore 90 with Montreal, Washington, and Phoenix. In Ottawa, he tried for 90 but the Senators had a rule that no one could have a number higher than the goalie, so he was given 28.

"It felt very awkward," he says. "I felt very uncomfortable not to have the number I wanted. I switched to 39 halfway through the season. I asked for 49, but they [GM Marshall Johnston] came back and said 39 because the goalie at the time, Patrick Lalime, had 40."

GILLIES
LISEN

Says:

"When he came to Montreal he wasn't the Joe Juneau who had scored all those points. A good solid hockey player and I think he was a very honest hockey player. He earned his money. He gave his employer, from what I could see in the games he played in Montreal, good value for the dollar."

Dick Irvin

Bet You Forgot

Only two players had worn No. 90 in the NHL until Enver Lisin wore it for 17 games as a rookie in 2006–07 with the Phoenix Coyotes. The Russian winger was the Coyotes third pick, 50th overall, in 2004. He had a goal and an assist.

No. 90

1. **Joe Juneau**, Montreal Canadiens
2. **Clark Gillies**, Buffalo Sabres
3. **Enver Lisen**, Phoenix Coyotes

Clark Gillies

Sergei Fedorov

During his 13 seasons with the Detroit Red Wings, the talented Sergei Fedorov played in the shadow of captain Steve Yzerman. But that wasn't an entirely bad thing, because in many ways it eased the pressure on the Russian centre; besides, he idolized Yzerman.

And that is part of why he wears 91, it being the reverse of Yzerman's number 19. But it partially represented the year in which he joined the Red Wings, the 1990-91 season. When reminded that he actually started in Detroit, after four seasons with CSKA Moscow, in 1990, Fedorov says: "It's not how you start, it's how you finish and the season finished in 1991."

Sounds logical.

Fedorov, who played on a line with Pavel Bure and Alex Mogilny in Russia and was drafted 74th overall in 1989, was a force with the Red Wings. He arrived, as mentioned, in 1990, after defecting from the Goodwill Games in Seattle. He has had 10 seasons in which he scored 30 or more goals and twice surpassed 100 points.

His best season was 1993-94, when he finished second in scoring with 56 goals and 120 points, but became the first European-trained player to win the Hart Trophy and also won the Lester B. Pearson and Selke Trophies, the latter a reflection of the completeness of his game. Interestingly, that season Yzerman played just 58 games because of injuries, allowing Fedorov out from the shadow.

Fedorov won a second Selke Trophy and wound up winning the Stanley Cup three times, proving himself to be a big-time playoff performer, with four straight springs with 20 or more points in the post-season. He signed in Anaheim as a free agent in 2003. He only spent one season with the Ducks before being moved, five games into the 2005-06 season, to Columbus where, like his days in Detroit, the gifted centre has occasionally been used on defence.

No. 91

1. **Sergei Fedorov**, Detroit Red Wings
2. **Butch Goring**, New York Islanders
3. **Marc Savard**, Boston Bruins
4. **Alexandre Daigle**, Ottawa Senators
5. **Kris Draper**, Winnipeg Jets
6. **Oleg Saprykin**, Phoenix Coyotes
7. **Jan Caloun**, San Jose Sharks

HOCKEY NIGHT

Says:

"He's a great hockey player. He has great stickhandling ability and he could see the ice in all aspects of the game. He was always dangerous, but unfortunately didn't come to the rink every night."

Bob Cole

Alexandre Daigle

Butch Goring

Bet You Forgot

Touted as a franchise player, Alexandre Daigle became a franchise joke after the Ottawa Senators selected him first overall in the 1993 entry draft. The Senators promptly signed him to the richest rookie contract in NHL history, a reward he never came close to earning. The number Daigle wore has such a stigma attached to it that when Oleg Saprykin arrived via trade from Phoenix in 2007, he was convinced to change from the No. 91 he wore with the Coyotes to No. 61.

Rick Tocchet

Hard-nosed with soft hands, Rick Tocchet was the kind of player coaches loved.

Philadelphia's fifth pick, 121st overall in the 1983 Entry Draft, the Toronto native joined the Flyers in the 1984-85 season and went to the finals that spring, losing to Edmonton. Two years later, the Flyers played the Oilers again in the final and lost, but Tocchet had established himself as one of the top power forwards in the game, scoring 11 goals and 21 points in 26 playoff games that year. Tocchet thrived in Philadelphia, wearing number 22 and scoring 45 goals in 1988-89 and 96 points the following season.

However, with a Stanley Cup continuing to elude the Flyers, Tocchet was traded to Pittsburgh in the 1991-92 season and helped the Penguins repeat as Cup champions. With his number 22 worn by Paul Stanton, Tocchet switched to 92—the year of his trade—but returned to 22 the following season when he scored a career-high 48 goals.

Tocchet would only wear those two numbers in his 18 seasons, switching back and forth depending on what was available.

He retired in 2002 having played more than 1,144 NHL games and amassing 952 points.

Says:

"He was in the Cam Neely mould, a power forward, tough as nails. I like to tell the story about the time in Pittsburgh, [Jaromir] Jagr was making fun of the guy and how much he was making. Tocchet told him to stop, he didn't; next thing—bang. He was a real leader. He could play tough, score goals, and he lasted a long time. I would have loved to see him and

NICHOLLS O'NEILL RADIVOJEVI NYLANDER MALAKHOV

No. 92

1. **Rick Tocchet**, Pittsburgh Penguins
2. **Bernie Nicholls**, Chicago Blackhawks
3. **Michael Nylander**, Calgary Flames
4. **Jeff O'Neill**, Hartford Whalers/Carolina Hurricanes
5. **Vladimir Malakhov**, New York Islanders
6. **Branko Radivojevic**, Minnesota Wild
7. **Aaron Gavey**, Tampa Bay Lightning

Michael Nylander

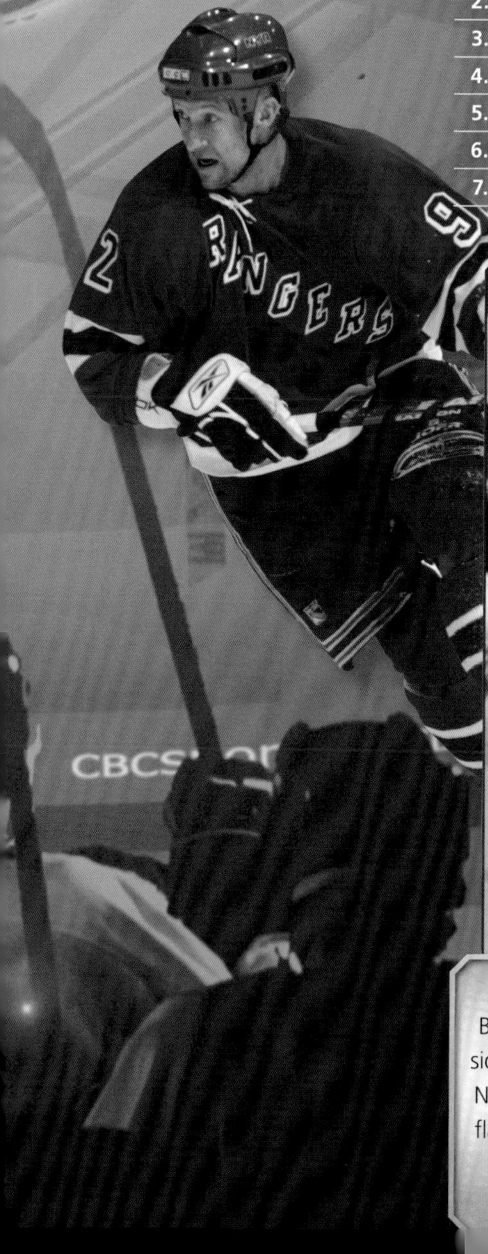

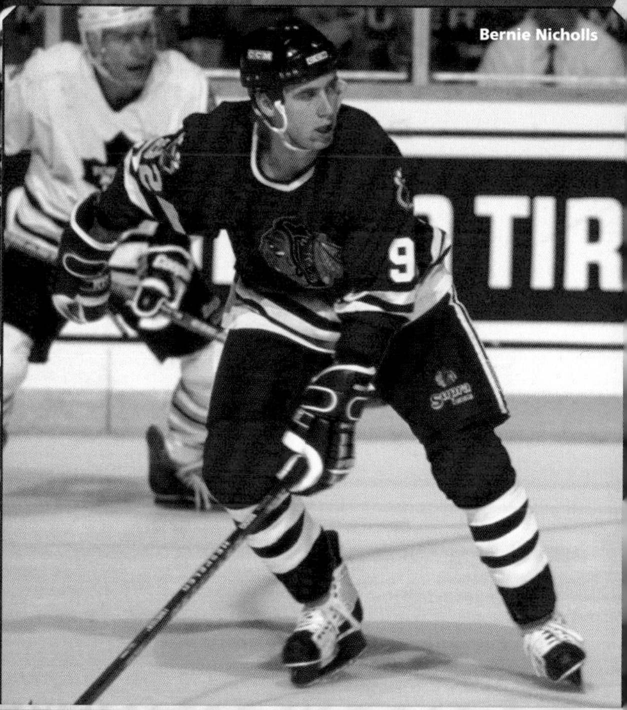

Bernie Nicholls

Bet You Forgot

Bernie Nicholls may have come from a small community (just out- side Haliburton, Ontario) but he was all big city when he got to th NHL. A flamboyant personality off the ice, Nicholls was terrific and flashy on the ice. He wore 9 for most of his career, beginning with LA, but switched briefly to 19 in New Jersey and 92 while with Chicago because 9 was retired in honour of Bobby Hull.

Doug Gilmour

When it came to numbers, Doug Gilmour didn't always get his way.

"When I was in junior, with Cornwall, I wore number 9," says Gilmour. "When I got drafted [134th overall in 1982] and went to St. Louis, my first year they gave me number 18. I had no choice with that one. Perry Turnbull was there and he had number 9. When he got traded, I got the number.

"When I got traded to Calgary, some guy with a big moustache [Lanny McDonald] had 9. A guy with a big nose [Tim Hunter] had 19, a big guy [Joel Otto] had 29, a lot of the good numbers were filled. Number 3 had always been my lucky number, so I put it with 9 and wore 39.

"It's funny, but in the summer, when I was with Calgary, I ran into one of the Leafs' trainers and I joked with him, 'Tell [Alexander] Godynyuk to get rid of 93 because that's going to be my number when I get there. True story. So that season the trade happens and he's part of the deal.'"

And that's when the old numbers game started turning in Gilmour's favour and he took his career to another level. Gilmour was a terrific two-way player during his five seasons in St. Louis, learning the defensive side of the game. His breakout year was 1986-87 when he recorded 105 points. He was a big point producer in his four seasons in Calgary, but he absolutely owned Toronto when he arrived in 1992 as the key part of a 10-player trade.

"Toronto wanted to give me 14, but I said there's no way I can wear that number [out of respect for Dave Keon]," says Gilmour. "So I took 93."

There was a story going around that the Leafs coach at the time, Tom Watt, didn't like big numbers, which is why 14 was offered. He was adamant that Gilmour wasn't going to wear 39 and when he told him it wasn't available, Gilmour said "Fine, I'll take 93," and it was done, much to the coach's chagrin.

Watt wasn't around to see Gilmour help lead the Leafs out of the wilderness and quickly make them a Stanley Cup contender, twice leading them with his heroics to the Stanley Cup semifinals, where they lost the first time (in 1993) in seven games to Wayne Gretzky and the Los Angeles Kings, then in five games the following year to the Vancouver Canucks. But Gilmour's heart, determination, and skill were big reasons why the Leafs got good in a hurry. When the Leafs were forced to rebuild and had to save some cash, Gilmour was moved in the 1996-97 season.

"When I got traded to New Jersey, [Devils' general manager] Lou [Lamoriello] tried to get me to wear 9, but I said no, 93 is my number," says Gilmour. "All the guys had a bet over which number I would end up with. Only Marty Brodeur won. Everyone else thought Lou would get his way, but I wore 93."

Gilmour went on to wear 93 in Buffalo, Chicago, Montreal, and for one last game with the Leafs, in which he blew out his knee, forcing him to end his illustrious career in 2003.

Says:

"For two years he was the greatest player in the world. In 1993 there was nobody better. At the end of the year, he looked like he was one step away from death. I could not put up a better example to kids of how to play the game. He'd do anything, take on big guys, he was a heart and soul player. He's a player I really loved. He was as good as Stevie Yzerman and tougher than him, so that's saying a lot. He was good on faceoffs, he could score, block shots, hit—he was the best."

Don Cherry

No. 93

1. **Doug Gilmour**, Toronto Maple Leafs
2. **Petr Nedved**, St. Louis Blues
3. **Daren Puppa**, Tampa Bay Lightning
4. **Johan Franzen**, Detroit Red Wings
5. **Anatoli Semenov**, Anaheim Ducks
6. **Alexander Godynyuk**, Toronto Maple Leafs

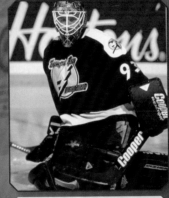

Daren Puppa

Bet You Forgot

Petr Nedved caused quite a stir during the 1993 playoffs. As a kid, Nedved had patterned himself after Wayne Gretzky, trying to mimic his skating style and mannerisms on the ice. That spring, while with Vancouver, Nedved and the Canucks lost to Gretzky and the LA Kings. After the final game, Nedved asked his idol for his stick, a move that was widely criticized in the media. Nedved ended up later playing with Gretzky with the New York Rangers.

Petr Nedved

Alexander Godynyuk

Ryan Smyth

There are two things Ryan Smyth very much wanted to happen in the spring of 1994.

He wanted to be drafted by an NHL team. And he wanted to graduate from high school.

At times, the odds of the first happening were infinitely better than the second. A ticket to the NHL was a lock, the other more of a struggle, but in the end Smyth attained both of his stated goals. He was Edmonton's second choice, sixth overall (Edmonton selected Jason Bonsignore fourth overall) in that draft, just about the time he was graduating from high school and completing a successful junior career in Moose Jaw.

As a result, Smyth chose to wear the number 94.

"It's for the year I was drafted and the year I graduated from school," says Smyth. "I dedicated it to my parents for graduating."

Smyth played parts of a dozen seasons with the Oilers, before being traded to the New York Islanders at the 2007 trade deadline after a messy contract negotiation with Edmonton, leading to an emotional departure.

In Edmonton, he is remembered for his grit and determination and his play in big games. While there, he broke a couple of Wayne Gretzky's records—20 power-play goals in a season and three goals in 2:01—and he became the face of the franchise.

Smyth also became known as Captain Canada for his numerous appearances with Team Canada. He played in the world juniors, winning gold, seven world championships (two gold, one silver), one World Cup of hockey (gold), and two Olympics (one gold).

His 60 games are the most of any Canadian at the world hockey championships. He has been captain of Team Canada five times.

Apart from 94, Smyth wore 93 at the 2007 all-star game in Dallas when Yanic Perreault got first choice.

Smyth, who was an unrestricted free agent, signed with the Colorado Avalanche in the summer of 2007.

No. 94

1. **Ryan Smyth**, Edmonton Oilers
2. **Brendan Shanahan**, Hartford Whalers
3. **Yanic Perreault**, Montreal Canadiens
4. **Sergei Berezin**, Toronto Maple Leafs
5. **Alexander Korolyuk**, San Jose Sharks
6. **Stan Neckar**, Ottawa Senators

Says:

"Pierre LeBrun coined the moniker 'Captain Canada.' He embodies how we see ourselves in the tussle."

Ron MacLean

Sergei Berezin

Bet You Forgot

Toronto Maple Leafs fans will remember this number with frustration; it was worn by the talented but frustrating Sergei Berezin for five seasons in the 1990s. Berezin's penchant for one-man rushes and shoot-at-any-cost tendencies eventually also frustrated management and he was traded to Phoenix in 2001.

Brendan Shanahan

95

Danny Markov

Daniil Markov, who goes by the nickname Danny, is a hard-nosed defenceman who has enjoyed a nine-year NHL career, playing most recently with the Detroit Red Wings.

Drafted 223rd overall by the Toronto Maple Leafs in 1995, Markov left Moscow midway through 1996-97, played half a season in the minors, then joined the Leafs full-time the following training camp. At his first camp, in 1996, he was given the number 60. At his second camp, with Larry Murphy no longer in the organization, he was bumped up to 55.

Markov had worn the number ever since in stops in Phoenix, Carolina, Philadelphia, and Nashville. But the streak ended when he signed with Detroit as a free agent in the summer of 2006. Ironically, Murphy had worn 55 in Detroit as well with great success, and the number was eventually passed on to Niklas Kronwall, who has worn it for three seasons. So Markov chose 95 instead because it kept a five in his number and was also his draft year.

Markov, by the way, is not related to the Montreal Canadiens' good, young defenceman Andrei Markov.

Says:

"Very competitive. I don't know what his lifestyle is like now but it wasn't very good when he first came over here. I think that got in the way of him maturing into the hard-nosed, rugged, off-the-wall defenceman who looks like he enjoys playing as much as any player I've seen recently. He's the kind of competitive guy who comes to work every night."

Harry Neale

No. 95

1. **Danny Markov**, Detroit Red Wings
2. **Aleksey Morozov**, Pittsburgh Penguins
3. **Michel Petit**, Tampa Bay Lightning
4. **Olivier Michaud**, Montreal Canadiens

Aleksey Morozov

Olivier Michaud

Bet You Forgot

Aleksey Morozov's NHL career began as spectacularly as a famous Pittsburgh teammate's, but the similarities with Mario Lemieux ended there. Like Lemieux, Morozov scored on his first shift in his first career game but, unlike No. 66, Morozov, who wore No. 95 for seven seasons with Pittsburgh, managed only 83 more points before returning to Russia.

96

Tomas Holmstrom

Tomas Holmstrom has blossomed into a rock-solid, gritty forward with the Detroit Red Wings, a player who is noted for his ability to take up residence in front of the net, to make power plays work, and for becoming a screen and a pest for opposing goaltenders.

Born in Pitea, Sweden, the left winger has played 10 seasons for the Red Wings, with his best output the 30 goals scored in the 2006-07 season. He was Detroit's ninth choice, 257th overall in the 1994 Entry Draft. He has twice played for his native Sweden in the Winter Olympics, in 2002 and 2006, the latter team winning the gold medal.

Holmstrom chose to wear number 96 because it was the year he left Sweden and started with the Red Wings. Earlier in his career he was a little too rambunctious at times and often took too many unnecessary penalties. One day, after practice, Holmstrom was asked by a reporter why he selected number 96. After he provided the explanation, Red Wings coach Scotty Bowman, who was standing nearby, said, "You should have picked 98 because that's the year you're going back."

"My first year, I was wearing 15," explains Holmstrom. "When Dmitri Mironov was traded to Detroit—he had 15 for eight years—he asked if he could take it. It took me a couple of days to think about what I wanted to wear. In Sweden, I had 23, 22, and 10. But those were taken and 10 is up on the roof (retired in honour of Alex Delvecchio). So I thought: 'OK, I'll take 96, the year I broke into the league.'

"If you asked Scotty, he said, 'take 98, the year you're going to leave.' That's what he said. That's a good scoop."

Holmstrom was also a good addition for the Red Wings and Bowman would agree. Holmstrom was won the Stanley Cup three times in Detroit.

Says:

"I think he's one of the smartest players because he understands his role and how to be successful. He's a guy that hasn't changed his formula and he appreciates and understands how he can be annoying and a real distraction for the goaltender."

Kelly Hrudey

No. 96

1. **Tomas Holmstrom**, Detroit Red Wings
2. **Pavel Bure**, Vancouver Canucks
3. **Phil Housley**, Washington Capitals
4. **Pierre-Marc Bouchard**, Minnesota Wild

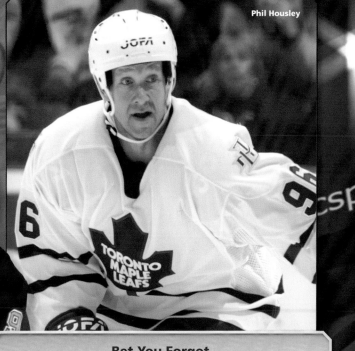

Phil Housley

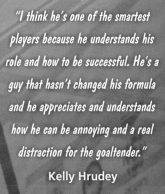

Pavel Bure

Bet You Forgot

You could make the case that Pavel Bure was the best player to wear 96, but Bure wore a few different numbers in his career, including 10 for several seasons in Vancouver and Florida and 9 in New York. Meantime, while recovering from a broken ankle, defenceman Phil Housley found himself on the move at the trade deadline when Chicago dealt him to Toronto in the 2002-03 season. Housley, who wore No. 6 for most of his career, took No. 96 with the Leafs but not for long. He played just one regular-season game and three more in the post-season before moving on. Number 6 was not available because it was retired in honour of Ace Bailey.

Jeremy Roenick

One word definitely comes to mind to describe Jeremey Roenick: colourful.

Okay, two words: colourful and outspoken.

On the ice and off the ice, Roenick has been colourful throughout his career, flamboyant on skates, outspoken in front of a microphone. Overshadowed at times, perhaps by the passage of time, is that Roenick was a very good hockey player and in many ways a good ambassador for the game.

A native of Boston, he was Chicago's first pick, eighth overall in the 1988 draft, which was held in Montreal. The night before the draft, as the story goes, Roenick followed then Chicago general manager Mike Keenan into a hotel bathroom and urged him to select him the next day. And so he did.

With the Blackhawks, Roenick had three straight seasons with 100 or more points, including 107 in consecutive seasons in the early 1990s. He twice scored 50 goals or more.

In August 1996 he was traded to Phoenix for Alexei Zhamnov and Craig Mills and a first pick. He had several decent seasons in the desert, before signing with Philadelphia as a free agent in the summer of 2001. Three seasons later, he was traded to Los Angeles and eventually returned to Phoenix as a free agent. Along the way, Roenick played in his 1,000th game, surpassed the 1,000-point mark and appeared in two Olympics and nine all-star games.

As a junior playing in Hull, Quebec, after a distinguished high school career at Thayer Academy, Roenick wore number 77. In Chicago, he wore 51, his training camp number briefly before switching to 27.

When asked why he wore 27 Roenick replies, "I took what they gave me."

It was when he moved to Phoenix that Roenick switched to number 97, the number he has worn for the remainder of his career.

"When I was traded to Phoenix (for the 1996-97 season) my son Brett was on the way. His name, by the way, was inspired by my buddy Brett Hull. I love Brett Hull. So, my first year in Phoenix and the birth of my son in '97 was all the reason I needed."

Throughout his career Roenick has been known for his great speed, his willingness to take a hit to make a play, and his inability to avoid, or his love for, controversy.

Says:

"After Bobby Orr, he had the most kamikaze approach to the game. Roenick cut through traffic as though he'd be able to talk his way safely to the net. I often wonder if he did."

Ron MacLean

No. 97

1. **Jeremy Roenick**, Philadelphia Flyers
2. **Esa Tikkanen**, Florida Panthers
3. **Rostislav Klesla**, Columbus Blue Jackets

Bet You Forgot

Though more recognizable for wearing No. 10, which he did while winning Stanley Cups with both the Edmonton Oilers and New York Rangers, Esa Tikkanen donned No. 97 in the 1997-98 season with the Florida Panthers. A fierce defensive forward with a deft scoring touch, Tikkanen picked up just nine points in 28 games before being traded to Washington and assuming No. 11.

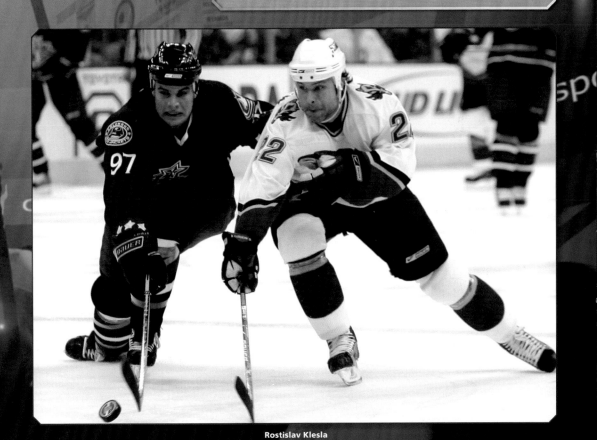

Rostislav Klesla

Brian Lawton

Brian Lawton still calls it one of the biggest regrets in his hockey career.

"Just one of the many mistakes I made," says Lawton.

The mistake was really an error in judgment. The first U.S.–born and trained player selected first overall in the 1983 draft by Minnesota, when he debuted with the North Stars the next fall he wore number 98.

"Nowadays that wouldn't be so bad, but back then the numbers were a lot more regimented," recalls Lawton, now a successful player agent. "There were no other high numbers other than Wayne's."

That would be Wayne Gretzky's number 99, of course.

Anyway, Lawton had wanted number 9 but it was taken by veteran Dennis Maruk.

"I wore 9 when I was younger, it's my favourite number to this day," says Lawton. "Someone

said I should wear double 9 and I said no way. Then they said 98. I took full responsibility. It was a terrible idea. Nowadays it wouldn't have the same bearing, but in 1983..."

As the story goes, around the league players gave Lawton the nickname "Notch," as in being one notch below Gretzky.

"When I was playing against Edmonton, some of the guys gave me a hard time and I just thought it wasn't worth it," continues Lawton. "I was a young guy just trying to prove myself and I didn't need the added hurdle. I'm not that kind of person and I never felt comfortable with that number."

Oddly enough, Lawton still had a decent rookie season, finishing with 31 points in 58 games. But he still switched to number 8 and later 11. He went on to play with the New York Rangers (number 17), Hartford (7), Quebec (17), Boston (29), and San Jose, where he finally got to wear number 9, before retiring in 1993.

"I always loved 9, for Johnny Bucyk and a plethora of guys," says Lawton.

Says:

*"He was Lou Nanne's great surprise—
and we were surprised all right.
He could have had Steve Yzerman
or Pat Lafontaine."*

Jim Hughson

No. 98

1. **Brian Lawton**, Minnesota North Stars

Brian Lawton

Wayne Gretzky

Interestingly, he wasn't the first player to wear number 99—he wasn't even the second or third—but Wayne Gretzky was certainly the best and will most definitely be the last.

That last piece of business was guaranteed on April 18, 1999, the day of his last game, when the NHL announced the number had been retired league-wide.

Viewed by many to be the greatest player ever, Gretzky had a profound influence on the NHL and dominated the league for years, writing and rewriting virtually every scoring record imaginable. At one point he held or shared 61 NHL records, covering everything from most goals in a season (92) to being the fastest to score 50 in a season, requiring just 39 games.

In Edmonton he helped lead the Oilers to four Stanley Cup championships. He helped put hockey on the map in Los Angeles with the Kings in the early 1990s. He made a stop in St. Louis and finished his career on Broadway with the New York Rangers. From start to finish he was the face of the NHL.

The story of 99, the number, is legendary, just like the career.

Gretzky's hero as a phenom growing up in Brantford was Gordie Howe. He wore 9 all his life—except for one season when he was really young and had to wear 11—until he got to junior hockey in Sault Ste. Marie in 1977 as a 16-year-old, and a veteran named Brian Gualazzi had the number 9. Gualazzi had waited a year himself to get it.

Gretzky tried a few different numbers, such as 14 in training camp, then 19 and 25, when finally his coach Muzz MacPherson suggested 99. At the time, Phil Esposito was wearing 77 with the Rangers and goalie John Davidson had been talked into wearing 00.

That is when he started wearing 99. He had a chance to go back to 9 when he arrived in Edmonton, but Gretzky declined—99 was his. Interestingly, at one time Gretzky wondered about shifting back to 11, because he appreciated the play of Gilbert Perreault.

But he again stuck with 99 and the rest, as they say, is history.

Gretzky's brilliance went beyond just his dominance in both the regular season and playoffs in the NHL. He was also a force internationally, first as a junior, then later in Canada Cup tournaments and the Olympics.

His final NHL regular-season points total of 2,857 will likely never be surpassed, not unlike his assists (1,963) and goals (894) totals. He won the scoring title 10 times, including seven consecutive years. He won the Hart Trophy nine times, eight of those consecutively. He also won the Conn Smythe twice and the Lady Byng five times, among countless other awards and honours.

Interestingly, according to the book *The Great One: The Life and Times of Wayne Gretzky*, when he was in the WHA and traded from Indianapolis to the Oilers in 1978-79, he wore No. 25 for his first game.

In 1999, upon concluding his remarkable 20-season career, Gretzky became just the 10th player to be inducted into the Hockey Hall of Fame without having to wait the normal three years. No surprise there. However, it was announced that same year that Gretzky would be the last player to receive that honour.

Indeed, there will never be another 99...and not just the sweater number, either.

Says:

"Nothing can be said about Wayne Gretzky that hasn't already been said. He's the greatest of all, no question about that. It's been questioned that when Wayne Gretzky turned in 215 points, that maybe the league wasn't strong, but every time Wayne set records, you'd find that anybody who was in second place was way, way far behind. Just like when Secretariat won the Belmont (to win the Triple Crown) the second-best horse was 25 lengths behind. That was the way it was with Wayne Gretzky. He was just that much better than everybody else."

Bob Cole

99

PAIEMENT
DUDLEY

Leo Bourgault

Joe Lamb

No. 99

1. **Wayne Gretzky**, Edmonton Oilers
2. **Wilf Paiement**, Toronto Maple Leafs
3. **Rick Dudley**, Winnipeg Jets
4. **Leo Bourgault**, Montreal Canadiens
5. **Desse Roche**, Montreal Canadiens
6. **Joe Lamb**, Montreal Canadiens

Bet You Forgot

Wayne Gretzky and Wilf Paiement are the two NHL players best known for wearing No. 99, but four other players also donned the same number. Joe Lamb, Desse Roche, and Leo Bourgault of the Montreal Canadiens all wore 99 during the 1934-35 season, while Rick Dudley wore it with the Winnipeg Jets in 1980-81. On April 18, 1999, number 99 became the only number to be retired by the entire NHL. Interestingly, according to Dick Irvin, he once heard that the reason the Canadiens had players wear No. 99 and other high numbers in the 1930s was because the owner was annoyed at the attention the football team was getting, so he had players wear "football numbers," as Dick called them, to help compete. Irvin said he's not sure if that's myth, but that's what he heard.

Wilf Paiement

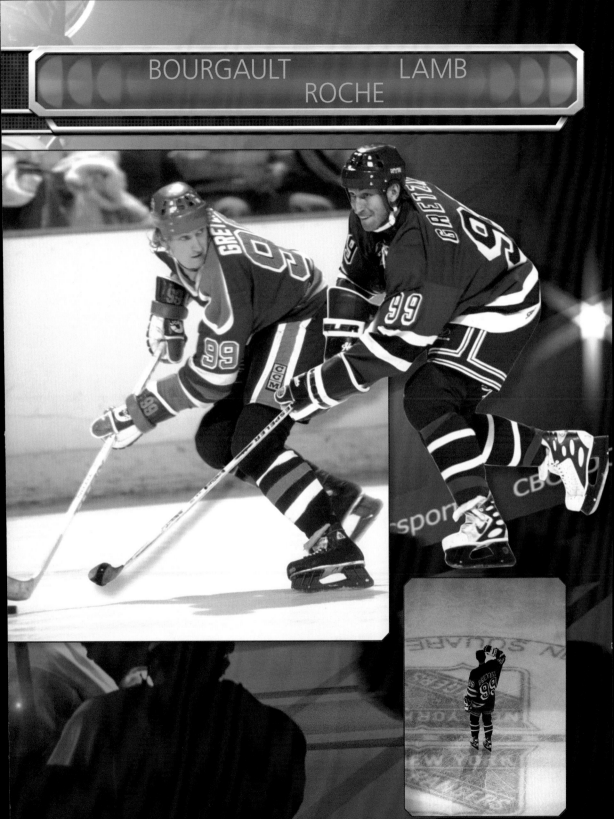

CASSIE CAMPBELL

A heroine of Canadian sport, Campbell took part in three Winter Olympic Games, and was the captain of the Canadian Women's Hockey team during the 2002 Winter Olympics in Salt Lake City, where she led her team to a gold medal victory. Four years later, she reprised her role as captain and won gold again at the 2006 Winter Olympics in Turin, Italy. She has competed in seven International Ice Hockey Federation World Women's Championships, nine Four Nations Cups, and the Torino Ice Tournament, amongst other prestigious match-ups, earning 21 medals in total including 17 gold medals and four silver medals. Campbell retired from competitive hockey in August 2006, and joined CBC's *Hockey Night in Canada* the same year.

DON CHERRY

Born in Kingston, Ontario, Cherry played hockey for the Barrie Flyers as a teenager, and, in 1955, he played one playoff game with the Boston Bruins. He spent the next 16 years in the minors. In 1974 he was hired as head coach of the Boston Bruins. Cherry's Bruins finished first in their division four seasons in a row, and he was named the NHL Coach of the Year in the 1975-76 season. That same year, he was named assistant coach of Team Canada. In 1979, Cherry's stint as the Bruins' head coach came to an end and he was hired by the Colorado Rockies for the 1979-80 season. In what has become an important tradition for Canadian hockey fans, Cherry has been appearing on "Coach's Corner" alongside host Ron MacLean since 1987 (although the first "Coach's Corner" segment aired in 1980).

BOB COLE

A front-line player on *Hockey Night in Canada* for 35 years, Bob Cole was inducted into the Hockey Hall of Fame in 1996 and has been honoured with the Foster Hewitt Memorial Award for excellence in hockey broadcasting. During the Team Canada–Soviet Union summit in 1972, Hewitt made the famous call of Paul Henderson's winning goal on TV— while Cole did the same on radio. The next year, *Hockey Night in Canada* producer Ralph Mellanby asked Cole to join announcers Danny Gallivan and Bill Hewitt. When Hewitt retired, Cole became the play-by-play announcer. In 1985, Cole and game analyst Harry Neale joined forces, and continue to be one of hockey's strongest on-air teams.

ERIC DUHATSCHEK

Eric Duhatschek, commentator on *Hockey Night in Canada*'s popular "Satellite Hotstove" segment, was the winner of the Hockey Hall Of Fame's Elmer Ferguson award for "distinguished contributions to hockey writing" in 2001. A graduate of the University of Western Ontario's graduate school of journalism, he began covering hockey in 1978. He joined globeandmail.com in September 2000, where he writes a five-time-a-week NHL column. Duhatschek has covered four Olympic Winter Games, 19 Stanley Cup finals, every Canada Cup and World Cup since 1981, plus two world hockey championships. He is a member of the Hockey Hall Of Fame's annual Selection Committee.

ELLIOTTE FRIEDMAN

Friedman joined *Hockey Night in Canada* at the start of the 2003-04 season. During a professional broadcasting career that began in 1994 at The Fan 590 radio (where he is still a weekly panellist), he has used his reporting skills to break stories and file feature reports for high-profile events such as six Stanley Cup finals, four Grey Cup games, two World Series, and one Olympic Games. He was the play-by-play voice for five televised Toronto Raptors games during the 1999-2000 season; a radio analyst for Raptors games in 1997-98; and the "third man in the booth" and pre-game reporter on Toronto Blue Jays radio broadcasts in 1998. He was named the Telemedia Reporter of the Year in 1996. Friedman has also freelanced for the *London Free Press* and *The Toronto Star*.

GARRY GALLEY

Former NHL All-Star defenceman Garry Galley works as an analyst on *Hockey Night in Canada*'s regular season tripleheader broadcasts, and on Stanley Cup playoff telecasts. In addition, Galley co-hosts the daily *More On Sports* afternoon radio show on the Team 1200 in Ottawa and works as an analyst for Rogers Sportsnet NHL regional game broadcasts. A 17-year veteran of the NHL, Galley was drafted in 1983 and played 1,149 games for six different teams: Los Angeles, Washington, Boston, Philadelphia, Buffalo, and the New York Islanders. The two-time NHL All-Star also represented Canada twice in the World Hockey Championships and was nominated on two occasions for the Bill Masterton Memorial Trophy for Dedication and Perseverance.

KELLY HRUDEY

Kelly Hrudey works as an analyst alongside host Scott Oake for *Hockey Night in Canada*'s western broadcasts of the Saturday night doubleheaders. During the 1999 NHL playoffs, Hrudey's segment "Behind the Mask" became a regular feature and currently airs during the first intermission of game two of the Saturday night doubleheaders. A former NHL goalie, Hrudey also offers his intriguing insights and analysis during the post-game show, *After Hours*. During his 15-year NHL career as a goalie with the New York Islanders (six years), Los Angeles Kings (seven years), and San Jose Sharks (two years), the former Medicine Hat Tiger compiled a record of 271-265-88, with a goals-against average of 3.43 and 16 shutouts.

JIM HUGHSON

Hockey broadcasting veteran Jim Hughson began his impressive NHL broadcasting career in October 1979. His 23-year storied career includes calling Wayne Gretzky's final game in Canada at the Corel Centre in April, 1999, and calling an abundance of NHL, OHL, and AHL games. Currently, Hughson also calls play-by-play for the Vancouver Canucks on Sportsnet Pacific. A Gemini Award winner in 2004 for sports play-by-play, Hughson has also been part of several national baseball broadcasts, including the 1992 and 1993 Toronto Blue Jays' Division Championship series.

DICK IRVIN

A member of the Hockey Hall of Fame, Dick Irvin has been part of CBC's hockey broadcasting team for 40 years. To viewers of *Hockey Night in Canada*, the Regina, Saskatchewan, native is best known for his coverage of Montreal Canadiens games. In fact, Irvin travelled with the Habs for more than 30 years as their radio broadcaster, and has covered close to 3,000 NHL games on TV and radio. In 1988, Irvin received the Foster Hewitt Memorial Award for excellence in hockey broadcasting. Along with his award-winning work on the airwaves, he is also an accomplished author. His books include *The Habs: Behind the Bench* and *In the Crease: Goaltenders Look at Life in the NHL*.

PIERRE LEBRUN

Northern Ontario native Pierre LeBrun, commen-tator on *Hockey Night in Canada's* popular segment "Satel-lite Hotstove," has covered the NHL since the 1995-96 season. Hired by the Canadian Press national news agency in 1995, LeBrun also added television broadcast responsibilities to his resume, joining The Score television net-work in 2003 and the "Satellite Hotstove" panel in 2005. LeBrun received Sport Media Canada's award for outstanding sports writing in 2005 as well as CP's President's Award. LeBrun covered six straight men's world hockey championships in Europe from 2000 to 2005, as well as the 2002 and 2006 Olympic Winter Games, and the yearly Stanley Cup finals.

RON MACLEAN

Ron MacLean has hosted *Hockey Night in Canada* for more than 18 years. Throughout his 20-year career with CBC, MacLean's role has expanded to include hosting CBC's coverage of the Olympic and Commonwealth Games, World Cup Hockey, and the Calgary Stampede. MacLean has also travelled the globe on several occasions to host CBC Sports' coverage of the IAAF World Championships. MacLean has been recognized with eight Gemini Awards for his work with CBC, including Best Host in a Sports Program for CBC'S *Hockey Day in Canada* in 2004 and 2006.

GREG MILLEN

Millen, a former NHL goaltender, has worked as an analyst with *Hockey Night in Canada* for more than 10 years, and has also covered men's hockey for CBC for two Olympic Winter Games—Torino in 2006 and Salt Lake City in 2002. Millen began his career as a broadcaster when he covered the Ottawa Senators during their inaugural season in 1992 for Molstar; he also served as the lead studio analyst for Sportsnet and worked as on-ice reporter for ESPN International. Appearing in over 600 regular season games throughout his 14-year NHL career, Millen donned the jerseys of the Pittsburgh Penguins, Hartford Whalers, St. Louis Blues, Quebec Nordiques, Chicago Blackhawks, and Detroit Red Wings and represented Canada at the World Championships in Finland in 1982.

HARRY NEALE

Popular analyst Harry Neale joined CBC in 1985. In addition to his famed role with *Hockey Night in Canada*, Neale was the hockey analyst for CBC's coverage of the 2006 Olympic Winter Games in Torino, the 2002 Olympic Winter Games in Salt Lake City, and the 1998 Olympic Winter Games in Nagano. He received a Gemini nomination in the Best Sports Play-by-Play or Analyst category for his work calling the 2002 Stanley Cup playoffs. As a former NHL coach and general manager, Neale offers viewers insider knowledge of the game, uncovering the keys as to why some teams win championships and others only come close.

SCOTT OAKE

Oake joined the CBC in 1974. Best known for his work as host of *Hockey Night in Canada's* western broadcasts as well as host of "After Hours," Oake's role as the Alpine skiing commentator at Torino 2006 marked the tenth Olympiad he has covered during his storied career. Oake also hosted the *CFL on CBC* broadcasts for 8 years from 1988 to 1996; in 2004 he hosted the hockey docudrama *Making the Cut*. From the NHL's boardrooms to the players' locker rooms, Oake has interviewed some of the game's brightest and most intriguing stars. In 2003, his interview with Brett Hull won him a Gemini Award for Best Host or Interviewer in a Sports Program or Sportscast.

DREW REMENDA

Drew Remenda brought 15 years of NHL experience as both a broadcaster and coach to his work at *Hockey Night in Canada*. He began his career in 1996, providing colour commentary for the San Jose Sharks on Sharks radio. Prior to his broadcasting career, the Saskatchewan native worked as an assistant coach with the Sharks from 1991-95 and also spent a year as head coach with their minor-league affiliate, the Kansas City Blades. He coached the University of Calgary's men's hockey team from 1988-90 and worked for Hockey Canada and the Canadian Amateur Hockey Association. Remenda returned to San Jose for the 2007-08 season.

Photo Credits

Thanks to Craig Campbell at the Hockey Hall of Fame for the many hours he spent sourcing the photos that appear in these pages. Without his help, this book would not have been possible. Thanks, also, to Andrew Podnieks and Graig Abel for coming through with some assistance at the final buzzer. All efforts have been made to correctly identify the photographers. If an error has been made, please contact the publisher. We will be happy to correct it in subsequent editions.